W9-BPM-262
HDRAWN

Sturgis 70th Anniversary

Timothy Remus

Published by:
Wolfgang Publications Inc.
PO Box 223
Stillwater, MN 55082
www.wolfpub.com

Legals

First published in 2010 by Wolfgang Publications Inc.,
PO Box 223, Stillwater MN 55082

© Timothy Remus, 2010

All rights reserved. With the exception of quoting brief passages for the purposes of review no part of this publication may be reproduced without prior written permission from the publisher.

The information in this book is true and complete to the best of our knowledge. All recommendations are made without any guarantee on the part of the author or publisher, who also disclaim any liability incurred in connection with the use of this data or specific details.

We recognize that some words, model names and designations, for example, mentioned herein are the property of the trademark holder. We use them for identification purposes only. This is not an official publication.

ISBN number: 978-1-929133-96-0

Printed and bound in U.S.A.

Sturgis 70th Anniversary

Acknowledgements

At this date, as I sit trying to finish up an already late book so it can go to the printer, I realize there's a list of people to thank. The list is always long, this one is longer than most.

I should start with Ernie and Scooter, the best staff a guy could ask for. Though I'd never met either of them in person before, they showed up in Sturgis on Sunday and worked like dogs until the following Sunday. No complaints, no hassle. No attitude. Just, "what are we going to do today?" Scooter contributed a large percentage of the photos in the book, and Ernie wrote most of the side bars and much of the copy for the book's later chapters.

Next on the list is Mikey, a guy I met so long ago neither of us want to talk about it. In fact, I've known Mikey for longer than just about anyone still walking the planet. We've shared a lot of adventures over the years, not the least of which was my first trip to Sturgis. Another would be publishing a little magazine originally called *Midwest Rider*. Mikey is responsible for the first three chapters of this book, and many photos as well.

Sturgis is always a matter of meeting friends, both old and new. I'm pleased to count Colleen Swartz, a great photographer from Milwaukee, Wisconsin, as a new friend. Colleen spent a morning riding on the back of my Bagger collecting most of the In The Wind photos you see here, and then sent me additional photos from various rides and locations.

I also have to thank Ken Conte from Rise Above Consulting and Woody, owner of the Chip, for access to the Chip during Rally Week, and for sending me a nice selection of photos taken by their staff: Aaron Packard, Ashton Wilson, Kevin Karns, Matthew Becker. Many of the music photos, and pictures taken during the Freedom Field service at the Chip, are compliments of the Chip's staff.

Up the street from The Chip is The Broken Spoke. Jay Allen and staff, including Carole Mittelsdorf, gave us free reign of the place for the entire week and helped in any way they could.

Though Jay didn't give us photos of the goings on at the Spoke, Dave Withrow and Buck Lovell from Maverick Publishing did. They also helped with ideas and a map and I can't remember what all else.

Chapter Three, the last of our history chapters, seemed to call for something special in the way of photos from, "back in the day." Thus I put out an email to Michael Lichter, and I'm grateful to Mike for making a group of his photos available to us, the book wouldn't be the same without them.

For Hamster photos, thanks to Jeff Levy, and for the Glencoe photos I thank Sean Clark. For some fun camping photos, thanks go to Brad, you know who you are.

Finally, a big thanks go to Tex the pinstriper, a friend who bought and paid for the very first Sturgis 70th Anniversary book when the book was little more than a twinkle in my eye.

Closer to home, I have to tip my hat to Jacki, our talented graphic artist. For proof reading I have to thank my lovely and talented wife, Mary Lanz, and for paying the rent on time so we all have someplace to work, we all thank Krista.

Timothy Remus

Introduction

I always tell anyone who rides, or just likes motorcycles, that they have got to go to Sturgis at least once. Luckier than most, I've been to Sturgis twenty two times, and I have to say this latest trip in 2010 was a lot like going for the first time.

You see, I've grown complacent, and comfortable. Spearfish and the two lane highways leading to and through Wyoming have become my preferred Sturgis hangouts. I have my favorite bar (the B&B) my favorite Italian restaurant (Roma's), my favorite outdoor saloon (Stone House) and my favorite day trip (a loop to Devil's Tower and back).

Then came the decision to do an Anniversary book for the 70th. Well, it didn't make any sense to stay in Spearfish, so the three of us chose Whitewood instead. If the book was to be a Sturgis book, then that's where we would spend our days, with the exception of the side trips to Hulett, Wyoming, Deadwood and Rushmore, all part of the Sturgis experience.

Sturgis is always fun, but for me this year was king of a rediscovery of the energy and spontaneity that makes Sturgis what it is. When I look back on this most recent trip to Sturgis, a series of short vignettes pop up in my cluttered brain:

A couple dancing at the Knuckle on a perfect afternoon.

The pretty blond flirting with the boys at the Broken Spoke downtown.

Rolling scenery flashing by on both side of the bike as I ride to Hulett and Devils Tower early in the week with almost no traffic.

The line of bikes stretched out in front of me on the gravel road, part of an organized ride.

The Cluster-F of bikes and cars on the east side of Sturgis, all trying to sneak around the traffic jams and get to the Full Throttle, the Chip, and all the rest.

Bean're's face as he told me about his life and adventures.

The face, and especially the fierce eyes, of the biker in the bar as he challenged another to "come and get it."

The mass of people, all well behaved, standing at the Chip listening to Dylan and Kid Rock.

If you've never been to Sturgis, you really gotta go. The visuals and the energy are just off the chart. Hey, I just went for the first time and it's an absolute blast.

In This Issue

Scooter Grubb

Scooter Grubb makes his living as a stock broker, but it's hard to tell that by looking at his calendar, or his photos. After a week in Sturgis, Scooter made his way to Bonneville. Anywhere that motorcyclist congregate and compete, you're likely to find Scooter. A good bike builder needs to be part engineer and part artist. Likewise a talented photographer – like Scooter – needs to be part technician and part poet to produce consistently compelling photos.

Mikey Urseth

Michael Urseth, Mikey to friends, is a man of many talents. Here's a guy who can write a story, take the necessary photos, and do the layout on the computer. And if the computer happens to crash along the way, Mikey can get it up and running again without calling the 800 number. When it comes to books and magazines, there isn't much that Mikey can't do.

In This Issue

Colleen Swartz

In addition to her motorcycle photos, Colleen Swartz does pin-up and commercial work. Colleen is also part of a business group that does everything from typical advertising work to the fabrication of large one-off signs. In her free time (?) this total and complete animal lover donates time and energy to a variety of rescue operations.

Ernie Mulholland

Ernie is a Phoenix-based media consultant whose career has been involved with broadcast promotions, publishing trade magazines and advertising sales for several major inflight magazines. His occupation has allowed him to travel extensively throughout the southwest US, Mexico and Costa Rica. This was his first trip to the Sturgis Rally.

Michael Lichter

It's hard to say anything about Michael that hasn't been said before. His photos are awesome, his dedication to making those photos boundless. When the rest of us who call ourselves photographers are sitting down to dinner in Sturgis or having the first cocktail of the night, Michael is still out there someplace taking just one more photo, going to one more event with a camera hanging on each shoulder, a tripod in one hand and a camera case in the other. It's nice to see that hard work and talent do pay off.

Chapter One

The Black Hills

Where it all Started

Bear Butte was a holy place to the Plains Indians and their religious observances continue today. Later, it was the site of an Army base knows as Camp Sturgis.

People in the real estate business have an old saying that there are only three important factors in buying a house. The first is Location. The second is Location. The third is Location. The Sturgis Rally owes a great deal of its success to its location in the Black Hills of South Dakota. The Black Hills are unique in North America. They are among the oldest mountain ranges in the world, possibly 2 billion years in the making.

Around 60 million years ago the entire region we call the Great Plains was the bottom of a salt sea. Each passing season caused another layer of sediment to be deposited on the bottom. Tremendous forces uplifted this section of the earth's crust, causing the sea to become dry land. Fractures in the earth's crust allowed molten rock, or magma, to rise from the molten core of the earth. This hard, igneous rock now rises some 3,500 feet above the surrounding prairie to a height of 7,242 feet above sea level at Harney Peak. From north to south the Black Hills run nearly 100 miles in length. The east-to-west measurement is around 60 miles.

The Black Hills rise from the Great Plains like an island in an ocean of grass, and like an island in the sea they present an entirely different environment than that which surrounds them. The Hills are covered with pine trees; this gives them their name. The trees are not actually black, but in certain lighting conditions they certainly appear so.

HOME OF WAKANTANKA

The Plains Indians called the Black Hills Paha Sapa, and believed them to be the home of Wakantanka - The Great Holy - and still consider them to be the center of the universe. The

Early mining was done as shown, by using water to wash the gravel, hopefully leaving the gold behind. SD State Hist. Soc.

9

This is the Hoodoo mine in Deadwood, showing the ore bin, complete with long wooden shoots meant to fill the train cars. SD State Hist. Soc.

Shown is a troupe of Native Americans acting in Buffalo Bill's Wild West Show.

Hills were the site of regular pilgrimages by Indian people. They would gather at the foot of Bear Butte (just outside of Sturgis) to eat, smoke medicine pipes, see visions, and commune with the Great Holy. Some would say that the annual gathering of motorcycle enthusiasts carries on that tradition, while others of a more traditional Native American outlook contend that it's all blasphemy to Wakantanka .

The Indians who lived in the the Dakota Territory when white men first appeared in numbers were known as the Dakota or Sioux. They themselves were relatively recent arrivals from Minnesota, having been pushed to the west by the Chippewa. The Chippewa had in turn been pushed into Minnesota by the onslaught of white settlement to the east.

The Sioux nation was divided into seven tribes, or council fires: Mdewakanton, Wakpekute, Wahpeton, Sisseton, Yankton, Yanktonai, and Teton. Of these, the Tetons were the largest group and they spread throughout the "West River" area (west of the Missouri River) into what is now North Dakota, Montana, Wyoming, and Nebraska.

The Tetons were divided into seven groups - Oglala, Brule, Two Kettles, Sans Arc, Blackfeet, Hunkpapa, and Miniconjou. In the history of the conflict between white settlers and Indians, it is the Teton people who are most often thought of as fierce fighters. They resisted the advance of the white man more effectively than any other native people. In the popular culture of the 19th and 20th centuries they have been alternately cursed as "heathen devils", and praised as natural conservationists. For the most part they were a simple people fighting bravely to protect their homes and their way of life.

BROKEN TREATIES

In 1868 the Treaty of Laramie was signed. This treaty assigned a large area to the Indians, including the Black Hills. It was called the Great Sioux Reservation. The Army was assigned to keep settlers out. This held up for all of five years until 1873 when the legislature of the Dakota Territory presented Congress with two requests. The first was for a scientific explo-

ration of the Hills, and a second that the Indians be confined to another part of the Reservation and the Hills opened for white settlement. The Indians had no one representing them in Washington and the first request sailed through with no opposition.

In the summer of 1874 Lt. Colonel George Armstrong Custer led ten companies of cavalry and two of infantry into the Hills. They were believed to be the first white men to see the interior of the Black Hills. Scientists on the expedition gathered geological and botanical samples wherever they traveled. Custer casually mentioned in his reports that there seemed to be gold wherever he went. Once the word of

As the gold became harder to find and extract, mining became big business, as shown by this early photo of the Homestake Gold Mine in Lead.

gold got out, there was no stopping the rush.

At first, the Army tried to stop the whites from heading into the Hills. After all, there was a treaty that specified the Black Hills to be Indian land. For a while the Army even arrested trespassers and burned their wagons. However, their will to resist the flow was not strong, and soon prospectors swarmed into the sacred Hills.

The Sioux resisted and did a pretty good job of it. In 1876 Custer and his troops were wiped out in the Battle of the Little Big Horn. He faced a combined force of warriors from the Sioux and Cheyenne nations who had joined together to fight against the white encroachment. The great chiefs - Gall, Crazy Horse, Crow King, Low Dog, and Sitting Bull - had joined together to fight. They won the battle, but lost the war. Outgunned and outnumbered, the Sioux were eventually killed, captured or driven away. The time of the white man had come to the Black Hills.

THE WILD WEST

When tales of the gold rush in the Hills are told, stories of Deadwood can't be left out. The glory days of the Deadwood Gold Rush were a period of three to four years, starting in 1876. From the wilderness, the miners and their gold created a town of 6,000 people almost overnight. Custer's tales of gold being nearly everywhere where almost true. Many miners "struck it rich" using the simple placer technique that uses water to wash gold from the stream bank. There was enough gold available in this way to keep Deadwood booming for a few years. Once placer mining petered out, the boom days of Deadwood were over.

Deadwood looms large in the American consciousness of the frontier, largely because of the highly exaggerated (or completely factional) accounts that were the staple of Eastern publishers of "dime novels." The exploits of Wild Bill Hickok, Calamity Jane, and Buffalo Bill Cody were in great demand by readers in the East. All Americans were eager to take part in the Great Frontier, even if only vicariously. Well over a hun-

General George Armstrong Custer led an early expedition into the HIlls. His reports of widespread gold started the rush that drove the Indians from the Hills. He paid the price for this at the Little Big Horn.

dred years later, A Cable TV show of the same name helped to embellish and sustain Deadwood's reputation as a wild west town. To most it mattered little that Wild Bill Hickok was little more than a hired gun, that Calamity Jane was a drunken prostitute, or that Buffalo Bill never visited Deadwood.

If you wonder how important mining was to Deadwood, consider the fact that the mine shaft located in the foreground of this photo is set in the center of downtown Deadwood. SD State Hist. Soc.

Ned Buntline was a popular writer of "dime novels" and magazine articles. His exaggerated tales of Buffalo Bill's exploits astonished even Cody himself, but were extremely popular with the public. Buntline convinced Cody and another frontiersman, known as Texas Jack, to take part in a play called "The Scouts of the Plains". In today's terms, the play was a critical failure, but a popular success. They toured for a year and were so successful that Bill Cody decided to strike out on his own with a similar play starring himself, Texas Jack and Wild Bill Hickok, in 1873 - 1874. Photos of Hickok

Accommodations in Deadwood Gulch appear to be spartan at best. SD State Hist. Soc.

The iron horse of the railroads was not far behind the miners. The "1880 Train" still runs today. Its 10 mile route runs from Hill City to Keystone. The rails changed the face of the West, dooming the buffalo, and the Plains Indians way of life.

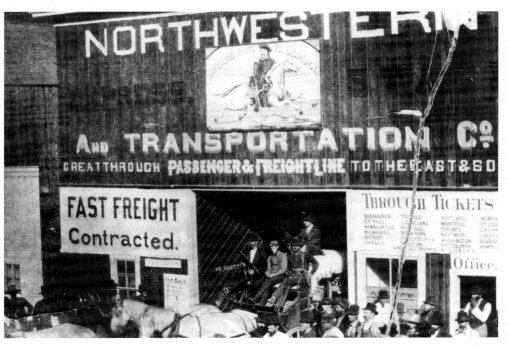

The Northwestern Freight and Transportation company was the biggest of three freight companies operating between Deadwood and Fort Pierre. SD State Hist. Soc.

and Cody together have associated them with Deadwood, although Buffalo Bill never visited the booming little town.

Life in Deadwood could be brutal and was often short. Although the pulp novel image of settling disputes with gunfire was overplayed, it was common enough. Indians often attacked miners at work on their claims, or on the roads, although they never mounted an attack against the town. Deadwood was a place where bad whiskey - or outbreaks of cholera and smallpox - claimed many a miner's life. But what a place! Some said that Deadwood made Sodom and Gomorrah look like a church picnic. Right behind the miners came the gamblers and the prostitutes. Many wise businessmen figured that it would be a lot easier to separate the gold from the miners than to separate the gold from the mountain. In the end, they were the ones who prospered. A survey of Deadwood's population in the 1880's revealed that only one in five of the population gave their occupation as "miner" All the rest were engaged in making money by serving the needs of the miners.

Among those '"needs'" was the desire for female company. In the early days, the ratio of men to women was extremely high. The female population consisted primarily of the wives and daughters of local merchants and the "girls" who worked at the local saloons and bawdy houses. Several generations of popular culture have softened the image of these "frail sisters of sin," and the "hooker with a heart of gold." The women who worked the saloons and brothels of Deadwood were a hardy lot, and if the photographic evidence is to be believed, a rather unattractive bunch as well.

The proprietors of the saloons were not always strictly honest in their "help wanted" ads. Many an innocent young girl was brought to town, only to find that her job description required more than waiting on tables or dealing cards. Many of these girls were led into a life of prostitution. One young woman, lnez Sexton, was hired as a singer in one of Deadwood's more notorious dives. Upon discovering that more than song and waitress duty were expected she declared (for all within earshot to hear) that, while her voice was for sale, nothing else was. She then stormed out of the place in a most theatrical manner. A patron of the saloon, one Colonel Cornell, witnessed her performance and loaned her money to stay at a respectable hotel. (One can only speculate at the good Colonel's motives.) A group of the "good ladies" in town held a benefit to provide Inez stage fare home. Most of the others were not so lucky.

Some of the best known of the lower dives

Not quite the real thing, these modern day "bawdy girls" in one of Deadwood's saloons are likely much better looking than the girls who proceeded them by more than a hundred years. SD State Hist. Soc.

15

were the Gem, the Bell Union and the Green Front. The Gem, originally given the grand title of the New Gem Variety Theater, was the longest lasting of these institutions. Al Swearingen was the proprietor and his place was often maligned, but more often patronized, by the locals. Masquerade parties became popular in Deadwood, according to one local humorist, because Al's girls were so ugly that the only way most men could stand to associate with them was to make them wear masks. (The photographic record shows, however, that most of the local boys were not so pretty, either.) Although the Gem was reputed to take in $5,000 a night, old Al died broke – killed while trying to hop a freight in Denver.

Much of the whiskey available in the Hills at this time was a notorious rotgut produced by local distillers. It was reputed to be more dangerous than the Indians. A cause of death often listed in the local papers was "bad whiskey." The fact that it was illegal to sell alcohol on an Indian reservation was overlooked with the same regularity that the rest of the Treaty was ignored.

Not surprisingly, some of the saloon patrons got out of hand from time to time. The bouncers of the day used their large size and an occasional billy club to restore order. Particularly boisterous or heavily armed partiers were treated to a "drink on the house". Known as the "assistant bouncer," or a "Mickey Finn," this was a drink laced with chloral hydrate. A single dose was usually enough to knock out the offending customer. He'd find himself in the morning sleeping in an alley with a hangover of world class proportions. The "Mickey Finn" is the origin of the term to "slip someone a Mickey."

All of these outlandish activities might lead one to believe that there was no law in Deadwood. Not so! As a matter of fact, all of these things, plus billiards, tenpins, and desecration of the Sabbath were declared illegal in the Acts of Incorporation. However, the authorities chose to turn a blind eye in the direction of most of these practices well into the 20th century. Several of the houses of prostitution continued in business

A bird's eye view of Deadwood in the 1870s. SD State Hist. Soc.

into the 1980's, with little more than a wink from the law. This practice has supposedly ended, although it seems very unlikely that the "oldest profession" has been completely eliminated from Deadwood (or anywhere else, for that matter).

The "boom" days of Deadwood were pretty much over by the 1880's. Most of the easily mined gold had been extracted and the miners moved on. There was still plenty of gold in those hills, but most of it was locked up in "hard rock" quartz deposits. These mines require expensive equipment and large capital expenditures. Homestake Mine in Lead (pronounced "Leed") has been in operation since the boom days, and since that time has produced more than 40 million ounces of gold.

Today the mine is closed, although tours are available, just stop at the visitor center in Lead.

STURGIS AND FORT MEADE

In 1878 the Army sent a party of soldiers to the Black Hills area to establish a post where troops could be stationed to protect miners from hostile Indians. By this time the Treaty of Laramie was a dead letter. The Black Hills were filling up with white miners and the Indians were being pushed onto smaller and smaller reservations.

Soldiers were first stationed at Camp Sturgis, located just west of Bear Butte. Later they moved southwest of the Butte to an encampment that eventually came to be known as Fort Meade. A nearby town was established and named Sturgis after the soldier's first camp.

First stationed at Camp Sturgis, near Bear Butte, Army soldiers were eventually moved to a better, more permanent location - Fort Meade. SD State Hist. Soc.

Sturgis owes its existence to the Army post, and to this day many Sturgis residents earn their living working at Fort Meade, which is now a Veterans Administration hospital.

Early Sturgis was not seen as the colorful place that nearby Deadwood had become. Perhaps the Chamber of Commerce should've hired Ned Buntline to write up some outrageous tales about their inhabitants. One of the few early Sturgis residents to achieve real notoriety was "Poker Alice" Tubbs. Poker Alice was a madame of great repute. Her "establishment" in Sturgis was known throughout the Hills. Poker Alice was welcome at poker games throughout the Hills, although she generally adhered to the rule of not playing with strangers. "Might be

dishonest," she said. Her trademark was the cold cigar she chewed constantly. She passed away in 1930 and was said to be missed by many, especially in Deadwood. Her house has been restored and moved to a location on Junction Avenue on the south side of Sturgis. Alice had a reputation for honesty and humor. According to legend she approached the local banker for a loan to expand her operation and to travel to Kansas City for the purpose of recruiting some new girls. Alice promised to repay the loan in a couple of years. The banker, although concerned somewhat with the nature of Alice's business, made the loan based upon her reputation.

Another bird's eye view of Deadwood, this time focused on the business district. Close examination shows signs for the Tin Shop, Pawn Shop, Shamrock Saloon and Hardware Store. SD State Hist. Soc.

Alice repaid the loan well ahead of schedule and the banker wanted to know how she had managed this. She told him that although she had planned on the Grand Army of the Republic having its encampment in Sturgis and the state Elks convention coming to town, but she'd plumb forgot about the Methodist District Conference!

As South Dakota entered the Twentieth Century, the frontier moved on and life in the Black Hills settled down. Deadwood became the commercial center of the mining industry in the northern Hills and Sturgis became more closely linked to the agricultural industry. Meanwhile, tourism in the Black Hills continued to grow. One editor of an eastern South Dakota newspaper suggested that Black Hills boosters would nominate Typhoid Mary for sainthood if they thought it would increase tourism. Every little town in the Hills looked for a way to capture a share of the tourist dollar.

Deadwood found a way to trade upon its colorful past by promoting 'The Days of '76': festival and rodeo. Sturgis was no different. The local boosters tried a rodeo, but there were rodeos just about every weekend in nearby towns. The area was "rodeoed out." They even tried a frog-jumping contest. That brought a bunch of people with sleeping bags and lunch boxes, but darn few dollars into local businesses. In 1937 something happened that changed everything. Unlikely as it seemed at the time to greatly effect the local economy, Clarence "Pappy" Hoel and a small group of local motorcycle enthusiasts organized a dirt track race along with a little trip to Mount Rushmore. And with that the course of Sturgis history changed forever.

The infamous Old Style was just one of Deadwood's many saloons. SD State Hist. Soc.

Chapter Two

Pappy Hoel & Sturgis' Early Days

Good Clean Fun

S turgis. Today, the name is synonymous with motorcycling. Seventy years ago, however, Sturgis was just a sleepy little South Dakota town nestled on the edge of the Black Hills. Motorcycles were fairly common in the area, since Clarence (more commonly known as J.C. or "Pappy") Hoel had an Indian dealership in town.

Pappy was an ingenious and aggressive promoter who would go to great lengths to bring the virtues of his Indian Motocycles (yeah, that's the way they spelled it.) before the public. In those days it was common for motorcycle shops to sponsor clubs. The clubs would meet at the sponsor's shop and, naturally, most of the members would ride the brand of bike the sponsor's shop sold. It was through J.C. Hoel's efforts that the Jackpine Gypsies were born. It was the hard work and perseverance of Hoel and the Gypsies that made the event we call Sturgis what it is.

From today's perspective it would be hard to imagine a less likely beginning for the big Rally. A handful of local riders would get together every week to plan a ride or a race, and then head out into the hills for a ride of one sort or another.

One of their favorites was the Searchlight Run. As the meeting began to wind down, one of the members

Father of "Sturgis," Pappy Hoel shown in the early 80s with a copy of Minnesota Motorcyclist, a magazine that turns out to be the forerunner of the Sturgis 70th Anniversary book.

The Tour to Mount Rushmore - led by the Jackpine gypsies - has been part of Sturgis week since 1939. Today, the mountain retains its power to draw huge numbers of two wheelers during the rally.

An early photo of the Jackpine Gypsies. They're gathered for a meeting at the Cozy Kitchen Cafe in Sturgis. Date: 1942.

would head out of town and ride up Deadman Mountain. When the meeting ended, everyone who wanted to participate would meet at the Drive-in on the east side of town. (Now the site of the Phil-Town Motel) One of the group's officers would pass around a hat and each guy would ante up a quarter or half-dollar. This would become the "pot".

About this time, the fellow who had left the meeting early was in position on Deadman Mountain. He would turn on his flashlight and everybody down at the Drive-in would roar off into the hills in hot pursuit. Up the canyon they'd go, each one with his own idea of the best way to reach the Searchlight. The first one to the light took the "pot" There was a catch, though, the winner had to buy everyone coffee when they got back to town, so things worked out just about even when all was said and done.

On one occasion, the Gypsies were in hot pursuit of the "searchlight" when they realized that they were not alone on the mountain. Thinking that some of their friend were playing tricks, they crept through the darkness, trying to elude the pursuers. Suddenly, brilliant spotlights shined in their eyes and the Gypsies found themselves surrounded by a group of Game Wardens. The Wardens had responded to a tip that there were deer poachers on Deadman Mountain that night, but bagged a batch of Gypsies instead.

The Jackpine Gypsies took part in many other events, just to have an excuse to ride their motorcycles. Some were games that are common today, such as poker runs and treasure hunts. Others, like the reliability runs have more or less faded into history. Some were variations on a common theme. The Suitcase Run was like a poker run, except that instead of receiving cards at each checkpoint the rider would have to reach into the old suitcase and pull out an item of women's clothing, and put it on. At each checkpoint the rider's outfits became more and more charming. It must have been quite a "beauty contest" at the end of the day that decided a winner.

When the county fair came around, the Gypsies usually took an active part.

One of the acts that Pappy performed at the fairs was the flaming wall crash. A wooden wall would be built and the whole thing doused with gasoline and set afire. With the wall fully ablaze, Hoel would gun his big Indian and blast through the wall of fire. He contended that there was nothing to it... you just had to concentrate on hitting in the center and not let off the throttle. Oh, yes... don't forget to keep your head down.

One year, the local Chamber of Commerce boys volunteered to build the wall and to tote it around ahead of time to promote the event. Normally the wall was made of one-by-fours, as dry and as full of knots as could be. The Chamber of Commerce boys, thinking that their wall should be nothing but the best, constructed it from top-grade tongue-in-groove lumber and painted it with several coats of top quality enamel. The better lumber, plus the adhesive effect of the paint made the wall much stronger than normal. J.C. was able to crash through it without injury, but it was the last time he let anyone else make his props.

Races on the Sturgis half-mile track were at the center of the first Rallies. This shot of the parking area was taken sometime in the late 1940s. From the earliest days of the event, top racers came from around the country to participate.

For many years, the rally headquarters was Hoel's shop. Many activities, like this picknick lunch, were carried out in the back yard of Hoel's home.

When talking to the old time Gypsies, I got a sense of the fun they had with their bikes. At the center of so much of this fun was Pappy Hoel. He was the leader of the Gypsies and according to those who knew him best, you really had to hustle just to keep up. The world is full of promoters and hustlers, but what set Pappy Hoel apart from the rest was his selflessness. All the time and energy that he put into the Gypsies and the Rally was aimed at benefiting the community and motorcycling in general. He always went out of his way to make sure that anyone who came to the Rally went away smiling.

The races at the half-mile track were the main attraction at the first Rallies. The Gypsies got together for the glamorous job of cleaning up the track and grandstand at the Fairgrounds. Racers came from all around the Midwest, including some of the best in the business. The Rally Headquarters was Hoel's shop. A big tent was set up in the back yard and any rider was welcome to roll out his sleeping bag under the canvas. In those days Pappy was an Indian dealer and his shop was right at hand for those who had mechanical problems. The back room of the shop was reserved for racers to work on their equipment.

Throughout Rally week, the lights were burning in the shop 24 hours a day.

The Jackpine Gypsies riding to Mount Rushmore. Up front is a youthful Neil Hultman, who went on to run the National Motorcycle Museum and Hall of Fame.

Faces

Dot and Dick Fissette astride their Indian VTs. In those days women riders were a rarity, and Dot was often featured in the press. Date: 1950.

Although this sounds like a booming business for Hoel, most of the work he did at this time was at or near cost, often with labor thrown in for free. A lot of the riders and racers were operating on a shoestring budget. Without Pappy's help they couldn't make it home or to the next race. Soon, tours were organized to give people more to do when they came for the races. The Jackpine Gypsies, as host club, organized a group ride to Mount Rushmore. The most scenic routes were chosen and a lunch stop was arranged. At the lunch stop, Mrs. Hoel, known to all as Pearl, would show up with the family car packed full of food that she and the neighbor ladies had prepared. Sometimes a tour would go out and stay overnight at Hot Springs, camping in the city park. The next day another tour would go out and they would meet up in Deadwood before heading back to Sturgis.

For many years the Chamber of Commerce put on a free feed for all the Rally attendees. The Park Service would provide them with deer or elk meat that had been confiscated from poachers or had been culled from over-populated herds. Eventually the event outgrew this custom, but it remains an example of the kind of Midwestern hospitality that made Sturgis what it is.

Along with the feed came an awards ceremony. The awards were handed out on Friday night after the tour returned from Mount Rushmore. For many years they were held in City Park with Pappy Hoel as the Master of Ceremonies. He always did his level best to get as many people as possible involved in the proceedings. There would be awards for the Best Dressed Riders (male and female), Oldest Rider, Longest Distance in the U.S.A., Largest Family, Longest Married, and whatever he could think of to get a few

More early women riders, the Motor Mails have been part of many Sturgis Rallies. Here they are forming up for a parade, circa 1960.

more people up on the stage for recognition.

J.C. was ahead of his time in appreciating the involvement of women in motorcycling and he really liked the Motor Maids group. A good example occurred in 1969 when he singled out Dot Fissette from the crowd and presented her with a pendant made from Black Hills gold - honoring her as the woman rider who had made the most trips to the Rally on her own bike.

In the early Eighties, J.C.'s health began to fail. He went to the Mayo Clinic in Rochester, Minnesota for tests. Many Minnesota riders dropped in to visit him there. When the tests were completed, the doctors wanted to perform surgery. Hoel agreed to the operation, but not until he'd gone back to Sturgis. The Rally was coming up, and he wasn't going to spend Rally week in the hospital! He did attend the Rally, as always an inspiration to everyone. His surgery was eventually performed, but to no avail. He went downhill after the operation and we lost Pappy in 1989. His last years were not easy ones. He had good days as well as bad ones. Those who knew him well choose to remember him in his full stride; riding in the Hills or down on Main Street promoting his Rally.

Today the Gypsies are still active in the Rally. Their headquarters can be found at the Vet's Club, located at 868 Main Street, just a few blocks east of Junction. The Gypsies will have souvenirs, T-shirts, signups for the various Black Hills organized tours and the famous U.S. and world maps where riders can stick in pens to represent their home towns. Time has taken its toll on the original Gypsies, but today's generation is no less committed to keeping the Rally the best in the world.

The Vet's is also a great place to catch a meal, especially the buffet style breakfast. They offer a hearty meal that is fairly priced, with the added benefit of knowing that the money stays in the community. More than once, my life has been saved by the Vet's Club sausage, eggs, hash browns and a little "hair of the dog".

We owe a debt of gratitude to those who have made this great event possible: J.C. Hoel, his lovely wife Pearl, and all the Jackpine Gypsies. Without their efforts and vision, this phenomena we call Sturgis would not exist.

Chapter Three

Sturgis - from 100 to 600,000

Revolution not Evolution

Seventieth Ann-iversary has a nice ring to it, but it's a little more complicated than that. The first "Sturgis" event was a race on the Fairgrounds half-mile track in 1938. This event was sanctioned and drew racers from around the Midwest, including Johnny Spiegelhoff of Milwaukee, one of the top Harley-Davidson racers of the era. This is generally credited with being the first "Sturgis," but simple math shows us that 1938 to 2010 doesn't work out to seventy years. Since the events were cancelled for the four years of World War II (1942-1945), apparently everyone decided to split the difference and call 2010 the Seventieth.

The first Sturgis National in 1954 was won by Al Gunter aboard a BSA Gold Star. Presenting the trophy is the Queen of the Rally, Peggy Burke.

The Gypsy Tour was added in 1939 to give riders more activities at the Rally. Mount Rushmore was the primary destination for many years. Later on a Northern Tour to Devil's Tower National Monument was added. Today, only a small percentage of the huge crowd takes part in these organized rides, but the Jackpine Gypsies continue to organize and lead them. They are a part of Rally history and a great way to spend a day riding in the Hills.

For the first years of the Rally, Hoel's Indian shop was the headquar-

From the first Rally, to the 70th , Mount Rushmore shines like a beacon, drawing riders to nearby towns like Keystone, Hill City and Custer.

29

Group photo of the Rally participants, 1951. This is Hoel's backyard, and the tent that provided shelter for many of the participants. The party always included movies of hill climbs and races, and an award ceremony at the end of the event.

ters. They had a big old tent in the back yard that kept getting smaller each year. The fabric was in real rough condition and every time the wind came up they'd lose a little more of it. Any participant who wanted to camp out could sleep in Hoel's back yard... just throw down a sleeping bag under the big top. Facilities were simple, but bikers' needs have never been that hard to satisfy. A hand pump in the yard supplied water and Mrs. Hoel assisted anyone who needed to cook. Sometimes there would be movies of motorcycle races or hill climbs from other parts of the country.

For many of the riders, the high-light of the nights in Hoel's back yard was the "pep talk" he'd give. Pappy was a booster, an enthusiast who could pass his enthusiasm on to others. Even in those days,

Rally participants, "Muff" and Paul Love, shown in 1956. Simpler motorcycles for a simpler time.

before Marlon Brando and "The Wild One," motorcyclists were not considered "normal" He understood what we've all come to learn the hard way: We're all judged, no matter how unfair it may seem, by the bad actions of a very few. He preached that message to those camped out in the yard and they responded. Nearby Deadwood celebrates the "Days of 76" the

Hill climbs were added to the list of Rally events in the 1950s and are still an integral part of the Rally. today. Photo date: 1958.

week before the Rally. Pappy always pointed out how many cowboys had been arrested, how much damage had been done by the revelers, and how many citizens were trying to prevent the celebration from returning next year. He'd then point out with pride that none of "his" motorcycle people had been arrested and how much he hoped that good precedent would continue. By the time he got finished, all the bikers would feel pretty darn special and would go far out of their way to avoid problems.

In 1946, the big war was over and America got back to peacetime life. The

Another Rally rider from the 1950s, John Schneider aboard his Panhead. Note the fishtail pipes, some things just never go out of style. Photo date: 1956.

During the 1960s, more and more riders began showing up aboard choppers. outlaw groups began to exhibit a higher profile causing much concern among the locals and low enforcement authorities. Photo date: 1968.

Four riders pose for photos in front of Hoel's Indian shop in 1959. The dealership served as Rally Headquarters for many years.

Rally resumed and slowly grew in size. Articles in the AMA magazine and word of mouth gradually spread the fame of the Black Hills gathering. Each year the crowd grew. The official name became the Black Hills Motor Classic. The Classic Board was made up of local business and government leaders who would work together with the Jackpine Gypsies to promote and organize the event. In the early days, there was only the tour and races to worry about, but as the Classic grew, there were more concerns each year. Today, the Gypsies handle the races and the tours, while the Classic Board works on the other aspects of the Rally.

The 1954 Rally saw the first National race at Sturgis. The previous races were called "Classics" comparable to the Regional events of today. Al Gunter won the '54 National aboard a BSA. Sturgis Nationals were held again in '55 and '56. The 1955 Rally marked the first appearance of "outlaws" at the event. A previously unknown group called Hells Angels showed up for the first time. Joe Leonard, a top-notch racer from San Jose, California was familiar with the Angels' reputation and warned the Classic organizers to keep a close watch on them.

The South Dakota State Patrol gave the Angels the heave-ho and an escort to the Wyoming border. The Wyoming troopers picked up the escort and handed them off to Montana. The Angels were treated to a police escort all the way back to the California state line.

Wild trikes were part of Sturgis then, and they're still part of Sturgis now.

As the Sixties came along, the number of motorcycles on the road took a dramatic increase. By the late Sixties, Rally attendance was approaching 2,000. The majority of riders on hand were of the "straight" school of thought - club members riding dressers and dressed in a conservative style. The police reported no arrests during the Rally. A few "hippie-type" bikers were reported, much to the displeasure of the local authorities. They were shown the fast way out of town by the police, because that's the way it was done in those days.

The big growth of the Rally occurred in the Seventies. There are a number of explanations: Baby Boom generation coming of age, vets returning from Viet Nam, Peter Fonda's "Easy Rider" movie, and more. Gunner Early, proprietor of Gunner's Lounge on Main Street had his own theory. In 1972 the CBS Evening News ran a short presentation on the Sturgis phe-

As the Rally grew, Main Street became a bigger and bigger part of the action, and the attraction.

33

nomena. They sent a top camera crew and reporters who had worked together in Viet Nam. Although not an exhaustive analysis, it was apparently powerful, since the crowds began to grow more rapidly from that time forward.

Word of Sturgis had gotten into the mainstream of American life and things would never be quite the same. It's been said that the turmoil that was part of the Sixties never really came to Sturgis. The reality seems to be that Sturgis, like most of the Midwest, didn't hit the Sixties until the Seventies. And like so many aspects of America in that era, the Seventies at Sturgis was a clash over values, beliefs, and power that inflamed passions and provoked violence. Presence of the "outlaw" groups hung heavy over the Rallies for many years. The "one-

percenters" maintained a high profile and made many people nervous, especially the local law enforcement officials. The Angels and Bandidos appeared to be on the brink of a shooting war for several years. This battle never came about (at least at Sturgis) and the damage to the Rally was avoided.

More and more of the new riders in to Sturgis rode "choppers," the cut down and modified versions of the big touring rigs that the straight riders preferred. They were also younger and affected the styles favored by the youth of the day: long hair and unconventional dress. They also brought with them some of the rebelliousness and disdain of authority that marked the era. This was the time of protest against the war and the Establishment. The

Back in the day, choppers were everywhere, including these on the corner of Junction and Main. Michael Lichter

Establishment responded to these challenges as it always does - with more rules and more police. By the Bicentennial year of 1976, the Rally had grown up. An estimated 15,000 were on hand to join in the celebration. City Park was jammed with nearly 3,000 people. There were extra police on hand to help keep order, but there was apprehension in the air.

Things went smoothly until Saturday night when some of the campers took to the nearby highway for some impromptu drag racing. Just to add a little spice to the racing action, bystanders poured gasoline across the road, creating a wall of fire for the racers to roar through. All of this was more fun than the law allows and a confrontation ensued. By the time it all quieted down, nearly 100 people were arrested and the fears of many locals were confirmed. Some local citizens began to agitate for an end to the Rally.

In '77 the crowd was again larger. More than 20,000 came to join in the Sturgis experience. The tension was high after the confrontation at City Park the year before. More police were on hand and backups were at the ready in Rapid City. Nothing happened. The event went off without a hitch. Some credited the six-foot fence at City Park with keeping order. Others say it was the weather, cool and rainy. Whatever the reason, everyone breathed a sigh of relief and hoped that the bullet had been dodged. Things went smoothly at the Rally for the next few years.

Some things never change, Main Street was, and still is, full of Outlaws, and Cops.

Slowly cruising Main Street was, and remains, a must-do part of every Sturgis week.

By 1979 attendance had mushroomed to 30,000. In spite of the increase in numbers, there were very few problems in '79. The friendly Midwestern hospitality of the townsfolk was perhaps a little strained as the crowds exceeded 30,000, but all was well with the Black Hills Motor Classic.

In 1981, there were noises in the local press that the event shouldn't be so big. The culture clash was evident, most of the residents of Sturgis are a pretty conservative bunch. The town is the center of an area of farms and ranches, and the quiet rural life the residents love was being disrupted, if only for a few days a year. Complaints increased from local religious leaders about the dress (or lack of it) and the behavior of some of the motorcyclists. The per-

centage of those coming to Sturgis just to "party" increased drastically. City Park was over-crowded and there was concern about the safety of the campers. In spite of all these concerns, 1981 came and went with only minor problems. In 1982 the authorities in Deadwood made it clear that they weren't happy about all the bikers descending on their town. Deadwood had become the place for the outlaw types to gather during the Rally. In order to discourage the outlaw presence, motorcycle parking was banned on Main Street. This lead to a call by bikers to boycott Deadwood. "Deadwood Sucks" pins and patches were hot items with Main Street vendors.

In spite of having no serious troubles in '81, Sturgis city officials were still concerned. Several

Looking at this photo from early morning, it's not too hard to imagine why the locals were a little freaked out by some of the things that went on in City Park. Michael Lichter

changes were made at City Park, including restricting the number of campers to 2,500 and doubling the camping fee from $2 to $4. A fence was installed to cut the park in half, hopefully reducing campground drag racing activity. The city also added brighter lights and provided for increased police patrols through the camping area. Weather was cool and wet through much of the week and attendance was a little down as a result. Many of the changes at the City Park were unpopular with campers. Bikers saw the new rules as a "police state." The strict rules of "no visitors" was designed to make the place less rowdy, but only succeeded in provoking confrontations between police and bikers. A move to boycott City Park had little effect.

Things wound up getting very much out of hand. Outhouses were burned. Gates were torn out. Crosses were burned in the park. The ticket booths had to be hauled away by City crews before they were torched. It was an ugly scene. Police officials made statements intimating that the entire city had been near destruction. A grim-

Gauging from the price of T-shirts, you might guess this photo to be from about 1979, and you would be right on.

A new set of rules was devised to keep things from growing out of hand at City Park. Photo date: 1982.

By the early 1980s it wasn't unusual to see women riding their own bikes, but they were still a very small minority.

faced State Patrol spokesman said that his men were able to contain the damage to City Park this time, but he'd hate to think what would happen if he had to pull his men back to the outskirts of Sturgis. There was an outcry in the community, with some citizens near hysteria.

Before this most of those opposing the Rally were viewed as prudes, religious zealots, or people who couldn't stand to see others have a good time. Now they were able to recruit to their side those who were just plain fearful that the event would turn violent. The Rally was in trouble. A large number of locals wanted to make sure that the 1982 Rally was the last. On the other side of the issue were those citizens of Sturgis who could see the positive side of the story'.

A group of local businessmen, lead by long-time Main Street merchant Don Larson, organized P.O.S.I.T.I.V.E. (People Of Sturgis Initiating Thoughtful Intelligent Voter Education) to lead the charge of those in favor of the Rally. The opponents circulated petitions and were able to gather enough signatures to force a vote on the issue. P.O.S.I.T.I.V.E. worked to dispel fears of the voters and to let everyone know how important this event is to the local economy. The battle raged, but in the end the vote came out in favor of continuing the Rally. It was close… less than a 100 vote margin. There was one casualty, however. City Park was to be closed for camping. Although the City had taken in considerable revenue from this operation, the troubles at the park combined

Check out the bikes on Main Street, 1982.

with the political fallout were just too much.

Other changes were made that have worked for the long-term benefit of the Rally. Sidewalk vendors were limited, making getting around on Main Street much more pleasant. We all owe thanks to the P.O.S.I.T.I.V.E. group, for without their commitment there would have been no Seventieth Rally to celebrate. The closing of City Park had other benefits beyond being politically expedient. In

Then as now, it's always good to hang out on Main Street, just watching and being watched.

Things were different – where's the traffic? Michael Lichter

the wake of the changes, private camp grounds were opened that expanded not only the number of camping spaces available, but the variety of services open to campers.

The Glencoe Camp Grounds, out by the drag strip, had over 13,000 campers during the Fiftieth Rally. That's over five times more than the capacity of City Park. Buffalo Chip, by virtue of being outside the Sturgis city limits, was able to offer a wide range of entertainment, some of which is of the "adult" variety. Whether one approves of these doings or not, there's no question that it's been good for the rest of the Rally to have some geographical separation of the "straight" and "not-so-straight" activities. Out on the prairies, those so inclined can do what they want without offending the sensibili-

ties of the local church ladies and government officials.

Another benefit of the efforts of P.O.S.I.T.I.V.E. has been a greater involvement of local organizations in Rally activities. Churches and senior citizen groups have become active in providing services to Rally participants, especially meals. At first, it was hard to recruit volunteers to staff-these kitchens, but as the word spread about how much fun it was and how nice the "bikers'" actually were, more and more people got involved. Not only do charitable groups finance their programs this way, but many of their members participate in and enjoy the Rally in this way. These people can see that their community, as well as the motorcyclists, has a big stake in the success of

What we thought were a lot of motorcycles just doesn't look like such a big deal thirty some years later. Michael Lichter

this event. That understanding is critical to the long-term viability of the Black Hills Motor Classic. Through the Eighties the Black Hills Motor Classic grew each year. The fame spread by word of mouth and through the motorcycle press. The Forty-ninth edition of the Rally boasted attendance of over 100,000 souls. Many were first- timers who came expressly to scout the place for the big Fiftieth Anniversary. The stage was set for the Big One.

Estimates ran from a conservative 400,000 to over 500,000 bikers showing up on that anniversary year to party with their friends.

After the Fiftieth, numbers came down, but always exceeded the pre-1990 levels. Apparently, people had a good time and came back for more, peaking again in 2000 with an estimated crowd of 550,000 to 633,000 on hand to enjoy the Sixtieth. For the next 9 years attendance ran in 400,000 to 500,000 range, bouncing around in reaction to the condition of the economy and fluctuating gas prices.

Sturgis and the entire state of South Dakota braced themselves for the 2010 onslaught for the Seventieth Anniversary and they were not disappointed. The "official" count offered by the South Dakota Department of Transportation shows the count to be over 600,000 (including the Saturday and Sunday before Monday's official start of the Rally). These figures are even more amazing when we factor in the grim economic situation affecting the nation for the past three years. Truly, a trip to Sturgis has become something close to a necessity for a lot of people.

An overheard conversation: "It's hard to believe that so many people are here with the economy in the shape it is. But I don't imagine that addicts have quit taking their dope."

An often-heard lament is that the Rally isn't like it was in the "old days". Fact is that it's always been different. Whether you first came in the 1950s or 2010, it will be different the next time around. Enjoy it for what it is - the greatest party on Earth!

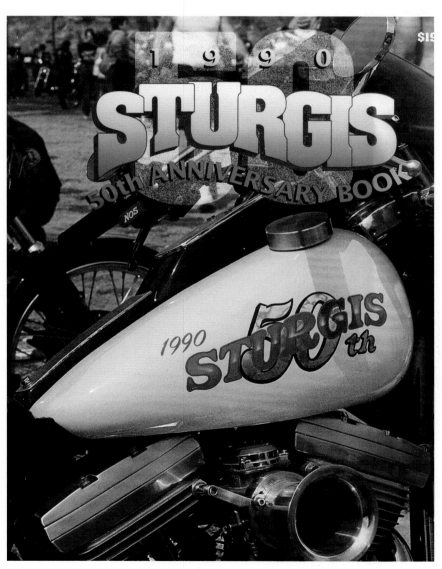

By 1990, Sturgis was far more than just a little motorcycle rally in the Black Hills.

Chapter Four

Events

Bike Shows, Burnouts, Races and Rides

Bike Show

Broken Spoke
Date 8/12/10

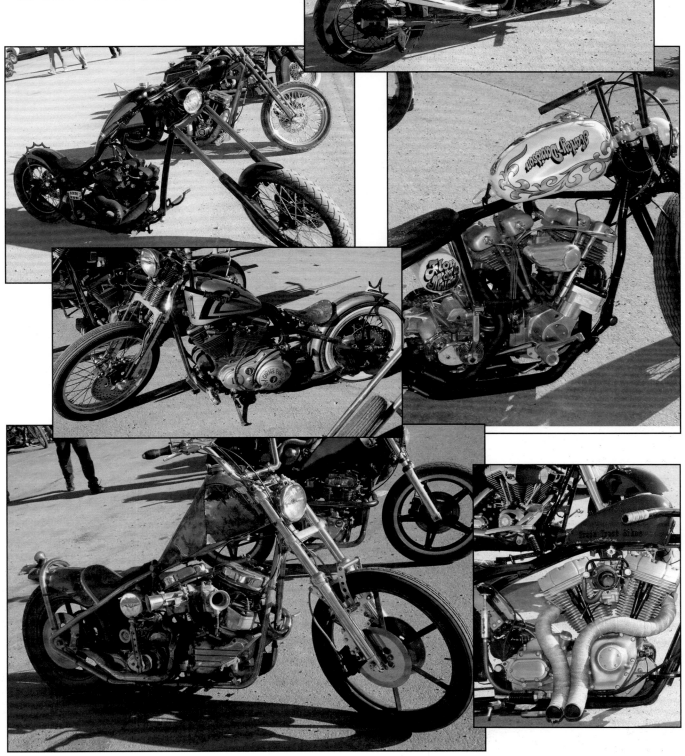

Cycle Source Ride

Broken Spoke

Date: 8/0/10

Bean're

Kevin Bean're
Carpenter
No Permanent Address

If you've ever wondered what it's really like to chuck the whole deal, the house payments, the car, the job and all the rest, just check with Bean're. When I asked if he had a permanent address, he explained: "I have a post office box in Tennessee, before that I lived in Miami and before that I lived in the Virgin Islands for awhile. A real residence is just a base, a place for my stuff. But due to the economy I have no stuff so I don't need a base."

Underneath the wild and crazy exterior is a very thoughtful and talented man. Clean and sober for twenty-two years, Bean're is a skilled carpenter. When funds get short he finds a job, often building and designing additions to some very nice houses. Once his part of the project is over, Kevin collects his money and hits the road again. The frequent travel gives Bean're an opportunity to visit rallies like Sturgis, where this year he found a semi tractor with an empty sleeper compartment – his housing for the week.

Our little impromptu interview ended with a discussion of freedom and what it really means. Bean're brought up Jack Nicholson's epistle on freedom from the movie Easy Rider, "they're not afraid of you, they're afraid of what you represent....." Bean're is the kind of guy who makes the rest of us wonder if it's really all worth it.

45

Burnout Drag Races

Buffalo Chip
Date: 8/12/10

Burnout Drag Races

Broken Spoke
Date: 8/13/10

Paul Yaffe's Best Bagger Show

Full Throttle Saloon

Date: 8/10/10

Wild West Rodeo

If you're looking for something a little different than what's happening downtown, if you like competition, and dirt, and a bunch of people having a real good time, then try out the rodeo.

You don't need a custom dirt-digger with a 200 horse V-twin engine. It doesn't take that much power to push a barrel or drag a tire. You do need a willingness to try, and the ability to laugh at all the fools, including the one in the mirror. In the end, it's all about fun and helping out the person you're competing against.

Wild West Rodeo

Rookie of the Year, Loran Whittaker

Of all the events that happen during Sturgis, the dirtiest and perhaps most intense, is the Easyriders Rodeo, held at the Broken Spoke Campground out on Hwy 79. Part tractor pull, part slow race, and part barrel roll, the show at Sturgis is just one stop on a multi stop circuit.

And among the pulling competitors, the ones who use their two and three wheeled motorcycles to pull a weighted sled, is one Loran Whittaker of Edinburg, Ohio. Though it's his first year racing his own machine, Loran managed to make it into the finals at every race he attended, and accumulate enough points to be declared Easyrider's 2010 Rookie of the Year.

Loran did all this on a trike of his own making. The scratch built bike uses a 124 TP motor equipped with a turbo, and is the first turbo-equipped bike to make it this far on the tour. Other than the paint, Loran built this bike completely by himself, or as he likes to say, "I dreamed it and I built it. Everything's me."

For years, Loran made his living as a self-employed machinist and welder, doing industrial maintenance and repair. At the same time, he kept a little part-time Harley shop operating at his house. A few years ago, when he moved into a new building, he decided to combine his machine shop with his Harley shop. Thus was born Evolution Machine & Cycle located in Alliance, Ohio. (www.evolutionmachinecycle.com).

"We do everything from oil changes to complete engine rebuilds and bike building at the shop" says Loran, "and I still run a full service machine and welding shop." Loran's unique and extensive bag of tricks gave him all the skills he needed to build a very competitive bike by hand - he placed second at his first event. With his first year's success under his belt, look for Loran to score big time on the rodeo circuit next year. That circuit is sure to include Sturgis, so keep an eye out for Loran Whittaker, a serious contender on the Easyrider Rodeo circuit.

Wild West Rodeo

Tire Drag Girls

Patti Foster, one of the official Tire Drag Girls seen in the nearby photo, says she endures the bumpy ride, the dust and dirt, for the simplest of reasons. "It's fun. Fun when everyone is trying to come in first. Even the dirt in the face is fun, weird as that may sound. Some people think it's better when it's muddy, because there isn't as much dust dirt, but I like it better when the dirt is flying."

The rules for Tire Dragging are pretty simple. You need two people, one tire, one rope and one potato. To make things really interesting, the organizers take that formula and multiply it times two. When the flag drops, the two bikes take off down the dirt strip, each dragging a tire, and the tire's occupant, behind. The riders can't go too fast at first, because the tire girl sliding along behind on the tire needs to grab a potato off the cone that's placed along the track. Once she has the potato in hand, it's balls to the wall. A drag race of sorts to the end. Getting to the end first is only part of the challenge, however. The rider needs to stop the bike, park it on the kick stand and get completely off the machine. Only then can his partner leap out of the tire and run back down to the other end of the track. The winner is the first one to drop her potato into the bucket back at the starting point.

In Patti's case, the rider is her fiancé, Scott, Neufer, and the bike is a mostly stock Sportster. "I told him to use my bike," says Patti, "because it's faster. But he likes the Sportster better, a lot of the riders in Tire Drag use a Sportster."

Though the Tire Drag is fun, it's not Patti's favorite. "My favorite is Potato in the Hay, it's more fun and less skill. It's like musical chairs, you ride on the back of your partner's bike, there are six bikes, going around and around a hay stack. When they blow a horn, the bikes stop and we jump off, and dive into the hay. There is always one less potato than there are motorcycles, so someone is eliminated in each round. We do that until there's only one bike left.

If this sounds like fun, take a look at any of the numerous Easyriders Rodeo sites on the internet. There were five stops on the 2010 circuit, and the plans are to add at least two more to the schedule for 2011 – so the show is sure to come to a site near you.

Tire Girls from l to r: Katlyn, Patty, April and Nicki.

Drag Racing
Sturgis Dragway
Various days

Michael Lichter Opening

Michael Lichter Opening

Colleen Swartz

Colleen Swartz
Photograper
Milwaukee, Wisconsin

The term is renaissance "man" and it means roughly someone with a wide range of talents and interests. A plumber who recites Shakespeare, or a CEO who runs a part-time welding shop.

Colleen Swartz might be called a renaissance woman. Most of us in the motorcycle industry know Colleen as a motorcycle photographer, one who shoots bike features and events for the various magazines. And Colleen is that person. The one seen shooting bikes and writing a monthly column for Chris "Wildman" Callen from Cycle Source magazine; the same one who has been the official Broken Spoke Campground photographer for the past 9 years. Colleen, though, is much more than just a motorcycle photographer. Back home in Milwaukee, she wears many more hats. Photography is always her favorite job, but it is not the only job. Colleen provides all kinds of photographic services for her customers who range from architects and remodeling designers to restaurant ownerss, bakers, and women who want to be immortalized in photos for their husbands. Product photography, pinup models, commercial work, fashion photography, charity work and pre-natal and newborn photography; the range of her photographic work is as broad as her interests.

Colleen's other hats may seem divergent, but in reality they all dove-tail together into a business plan that utilizes the talents of a group of highly talented people to provide services to their clients. When not in the studio producing photographic work, Colleen can be found in the fabrication shop building, or the office designing. JP, Colleen's life partner, owns the PCI Group, which is the parent company of Colleen's Photography business as well as Cook Custom's (best known as Dave Cook, 2009 AMD World Champion Bike Builder), and a sign and plastics manufacturing business. With work ranging from small signs for individual businesses to full decor packages to trade show booths and vinyl vehicle wraps, PCI Group does it all. Colleen likes to describe it as, "If you need something and you can't go and buy it off the shelf somewhere, we can produce it."

So between Sturgis and the next motorcycle event, Colleen can be found taking photos, producing ad campaigns, printing large format banners, building a new grocery store interior, routing plastic to be used in a point of purchase display, and creating a booth for the local farmer's market for a company that makes organic baked goods. And if she gets bored with that, she might just, "take off in my car, visiting motorcycle shops and friends along the way. When I get back home I sort all the images and sell the features to people like Chris Maida at American Iron."

Part photographer, part designer and part motorcycle nut, Colleen may not be a plumber or a welder, but she sure does carry a big personal tool box. One that contains the skills and the spunk needed to accomplish nearly anything, from photographing bikes and bikers, to designing an entire promotional package designed to make the potential of her customer's businesses evident to their target market.

Faces

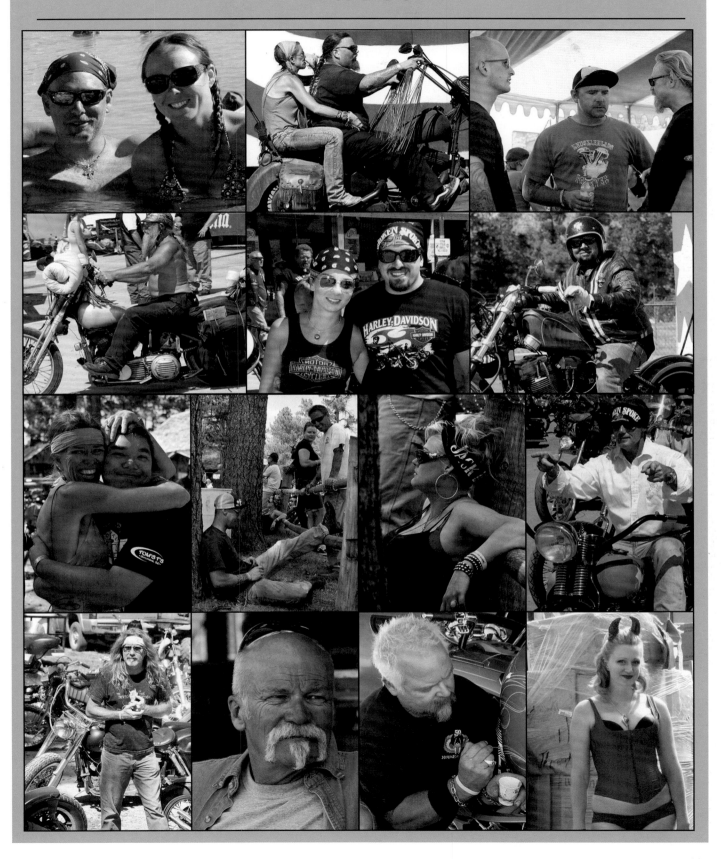

AMC Bike Show

Downtown Sturgis
Date: 8/11/10

F-ing Giant Group Burnout

At the Broken Spoke, they decided to have more than just a burnout contest, more even than the burn out drag races. They decided to have the world's biggest group burnout.

Whether they achieved that goal or not we can't say. We can only say that the roar of all those V-twins was hellaciously loud. And the smoke, well, the smoke was impenetrable. Oh yea, and the crowd loved it. From the bark of the first V-twin to the last wisp of smoke, the upper rail was filled with spectators, each one vying for a good look at all those crazy bikers.

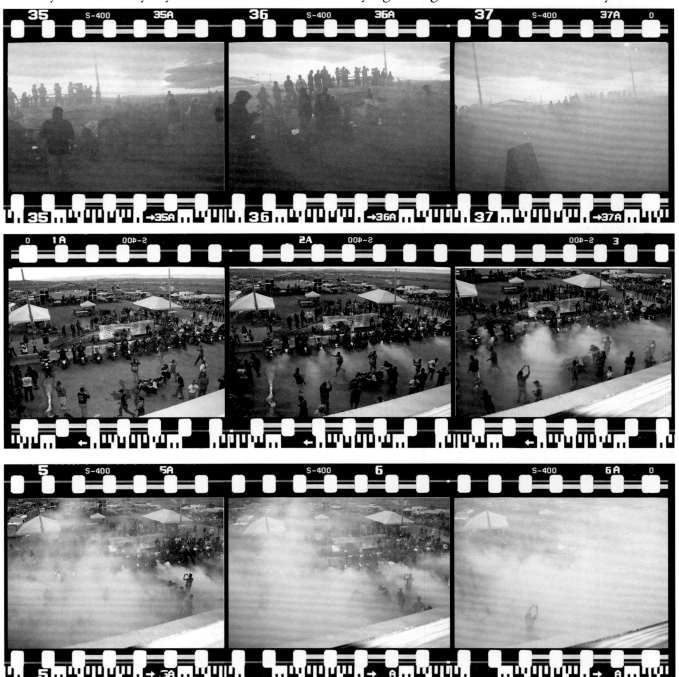

Legends Ride

Deadwood

Date: 8/8/10

Freedom Field

Buffalo Chip
Date: 8/8/10

Wall of Death

Broken Spoke
Date: All week

Hamster Ride

Spearfish to Sturgis
Date: 8/12/10

Chapter Five

Main Street

Nothing Else Like It

When you walk along Main Street in Sturgis during the Rally, you can't help but wonder what this likeable, quaint city, population 6,500, is like the other 51 weeks of the year.

The Rally crowd of 600,000 doesn't descend on Sturgis en masse. They're spread out in outlying towns as well as the campgrounds, large and small, on the outskirts of town. But any true Sturgis itinerary involves hitting the downtown scene at least once, because there's nothing like it. Period.

The one thing about Main Street, there are always people coming and going...

Just about any time of day the atmosphere is a cross between Mardi Gras and Superbowl weekend - with a little Woodstock mixed in - all confined within what reminds you of your favorite small college town.

Both sides of Main Street are crowded, so you dodge and weave your way along, eyes wide open trying to see everything you can. You elbow your way into one of the many bars, looking for a spot. It feels great to get off your feet and be out of the sun. Bustling bartenders are popping off bottle tops in rapid succession, and are quick with their pour guns. Pretty, wildly-dressed waitresses are in overdrive too, quick to take your order with a smile and a quip. It doesn't take long to strike up a conversation with just about anyone around you. "Where are you from?" "Is this your

...and others just watching the comings and the goings.

first time to Sturgis?" "Where are you staying?" "How about another round?" It's easy to make new friends, good ones.

You leave that place, and blasting classic rock music follows you out into the street, creating the soundtrack for the dream-like street scene that surrounds you.

Downtown is a people watching mecca. There are young and old, beards, shaved heads, tattoos, sunburned skin, halter-topped women (of all ages), leather fashions, dogs with hats, costumed riders, watchful cops, gawking locals, the religious right, the Hells Angels, and tourists from parts unknown. Look - there's a couple who just got married!

You look in every direction. The biker parade keeps coming ... and coming ... and coming.

Business is brisk inside the tattoo parlors. You look inside and see someone grimacing as they get elaborate work done, while another just gets a touch up. Others stand off to the side, nonchalantly flipping through tattoo catalogs, secretly yearning for a special design to seduce them.

And what makes it so special, the reason that all these people are here, is that during this one week motorcycles rule. Motorcycles are everywhere. They're parked in formations for blocks on end down Main Street, parked in alleyways and backstreets. Motorcycles are on display in exhibit areas, competing for awards. They're mixed in with artwork in galleries. There's even a museum of motorcycles in Sturgis. There's every conceivable motorcycle part or accessory for sale in the vendor tents that line the streets coming into town. Motorcycles are on the move, everywhere, flowing in and out of downtown all day long.

And with thousands upon thousands upon thousands of motorcycles, there's that unmistakable sound: a blasting engine burst, then a steady roar, and then that fading rumble into the distance. During this one special week in Sturgis, you wake up and fall asleep to fuel-injected music made by motorcycles engines.

There's nothing else like it.

Baby Burd & Scotty

"Baby Burd" and Scotty
Windmill Builders
Laramie, Wyoming

Baby Burd first saw Sturgis when she was only nine year old. She was on the back of a '49 Knuckle, hugging on to her father, riding in all the way from northern California. Needless to say, that experience left a deep impression, one she recalls to this day. Since then, she's been to Sturgis 23 times. Over the years she's brought along her kids - and grandkids.

This year is a little different, however. She and Scotty are having a good time together – just the two of them. "We love to see all our old friends. Mostly, we just hang around downtown. We're not into the other events that happen outside town like the concerts and the rides. This is social. Seeing old friends, and making new friends, that's what we like," she said. Scotty added "You know, bikers have a bad rap, but it's just not true. Let me tell you this story. Last night we pulled into town late at night with no place to stay. We ran into a local lady, Esther, who goes about four-foot nothing. Turns out everyone around here knows Esther. She's a local legend. So, she sees we're stuck and takes us in. We spent the night at her house and in the morning she introduces us to her family. Come on, you won't see that happen anywhere else. Now we have a new friend forever."

Newlyweds

Debbie & Eric Bruce
Newlyweds
Belton, Missouri

"I always wanted a biker wedding. What better place than Sturgis?"

That's Debbie's answer to why she and Eric decided to tie the knot during the Sturgis rally. Reciting personalized vows during their service which was conducted on a beautiful South Dakota afternoon capped off their whirlwind romance. The two lovebirds met online in early 2010, and one month later Eric proposed while they were inside his semi. They made the necessary arrangements from their home in Missouri a month in advance, then rode to Sturgis together on a 2003 Fatboy. Eric was a Sturgis "newbie," but it was Debbie's second rally. In addition to taking in the sights and marquee events in Sturgis during their honeymoon, they were looking forward to a ride with friends out to Devils Tower.

Debby & Eric Bruce

Sheila and Wayne Johnson
Newlyweds
Hooper, Nebraska

"Our kids wanted us to go to Vegas to get married, but we knew we were coming here and liked the idea. We're having a great time!" reported Sheila Johnson. She went on to say that "Sturgis is a pretty popular place to tie the knot. We heard that 40 couples applied for a wedding license just today. Now it's honeymoon time!"

As Sheila has been involved with the military and law enforcement,, they set the nuptial time at 13:00 hours on August 13. "She's ornery, that's why I like her," Wayne added.

Even though the couple rode 570 miles together to get to their own wedding in Sturgis, these newlyweds look forward to the bigger journey ahead of them.

Sheila and Wayne Johnson

Faces

Officer Greg Swanson

Greg Swanson
Special Officer
Sturgis, South Dakota

Special Officer Greg Swanson has worked the streets of Sturgis during every Rally for the past 32 years. You get the sense he's pretty much seen it all.

"Early on, they used to section off just three blocks of Main Street for the bikers. We thought that was pretty big at the time. Those people camped at City Park, but it was crowded and there weren't any proper facilities in place," he reflected. "It was pretty wild back then, a much rougher crowd with not that much to do but cause trouble. After the community got behind the event, things started to evolve. The campgrounds outside of town sprang up, more special events around Sturgis were scheduled to attract the business and all the different rides became popular. And so the number of tourists started to increase into the mix. As the crowd split up at different locations, it got easier to control."

"The fiftieth anniversary in 1990 was a big one. I remember the traffic being unbelievable. We had to ride our police bikes on the sidewalks to get through the crowds," he added.

As he stands off to the side, carefully watching the crowded downtown scene, one wonders how he deals with this wave of humanity that has invaded this normally quiet town during the Rally. "Well, I think that as long as people have a decent place to stay, access to food, entertainment and activities, they'll be happy and have a good time. That's what we want."

Kai & Detlef

Kai Rubow & Detlef Klein
Private Pilots
Swakopmund, Namibia, Africa

With only one million people in their native country of Namibia, just imagine how Kai Rubow and Detlef Klein felt when they arrived in Sturgis and encountered some 600,000 people in one destination.

These long-time friends grew up in the same hometown and got the riding bug at the same time. While attending an aviation event in Oskosh, Wisconsin, in 2006, they took a side trip to Milwaukee to see the Harley-Davidson facilities. They got hooked. Upon their return to Africa, they bought Harleys and have enjoyed riding through southern Africa ever since.

They heard about Sturgis. Wanting to add to their long list of action-packed exotic vacations, they decided to make a trip to South Dakota happen, kicking off an odyssey that would take them half a world away. After a 30-hour flight from Cape Town to Denver, they rented Harleys and rode to Deadwood to stay in a rented house. "Because of the travel time, we will be spending 27 days on this trip. Besides Sturgis, we plan to ride out to Yellowstone and Custer State Park. So far I would say the people are really friendly, very respectful. You feel safe on the rides we have taken," Kai said.

On this evening, the dynamic duo had made it a point to check out the scene at the Buffalo Chip and catch the Bob Dylan concert.

While the trip was expensive and time-consuming, Detlef said he would consider coming back — next time with his kids! Their only regret was not being able to take home as many souvenirs as they wanted, due to the length of their journey and baggage restrictions.

Dave Withrow

Dave Withrow
Publisher, Maverick Publishing
(American Cycle, American Bagger and Urban Bagger magazines)
Spearfish, South Dakota

Maverick Publishing is an impressive media operation with some unique twists. For starters, there's a full-service custom bike shop built into the bottom floor of their offices. And then there's the location - the facility looks out over beautiful Spearfish, South Dakota. Nice set up, for sure.

The on-site shop allows the magazine's writers, editors and photographers to have insider access to the custom bikes, products and other tech items they eventually showcase in the publications. In fact, about 90 percent of the tech photography seen in the magazines is shot there.

Again this year, Maverick Publishing hosted a VIP kick-off reception on the first Sunday night of Rally Week at their facility in Spearfish that brings together leading builders, vendors and industry friends. "It gives everybody a chance to get together and relax a bit before the Rally starts. We've done it for a few years now and it keeps growing. I think we had 600 people this year," Withrow added.

When asked his opinion of the 2010 Rally, he noted that "While the economy is still not good, the Sturgis rally still has its way of attracting people. After you have experienced it, you might miss going once, but not twice. I heard numbers were up, probably due to the 70th anniversary and the fact that different types of people come for different things now, like all the music and concerts. The demographics are changing," he added.

Even after the Rally crowds fade, there's still lots of action happening at Maverick Publishing year-round. "Surprisingly, a lot of our builder contacts and friends in the industry have bought second homes in the area. So we get a chance to see them throughout the year," he said. "We host a ride in June or July, depending on the weather, and we have a lot of fun then with everyone. They've come to love the Black Hills as much as I have."

From his position as an influential industry leader on a national level – as well as a local Sturgis-area resident – Dave Withrow continues to have an impact on the motorcycle world while positioning Maverick Publishing for long-term success.

Vaughn& Lori/Dave Zien

Vaughn and Lori Shafer
Bare Bonz Choppers
EL Jebel, Colorado

Four months before the Sturgis rally, Vaughn Shafer received an inspiration. The master blacksmith, renowned for his customized hand-forged sculptures and motorcycles, felt a creative urge to produce a work to honor our troops in Iran and Afghanistan.

Over the next few months, he spent a dedicated amount of time each day producing "A Tribute to Our Armed Forces," which debuted inside his firm's booth at the Buffalo Chip. Not only were visitors able to experience this unique sculpture up close and personal, they also had the opportunity to donate $10 to have their initials plasma-cut into the steel base of the work. At night the base was illuminated, which showcased the entire piece in a dramatic, stirring fashion.

What happens to the work after the Sturgis exhibition? "Ideally, I would like to find a permanent home for it. Maybe a military instillation or a corporate environment," he said.

Let's hope the right party will also be inspired enough to acquire this work and display it in the right place, for all the right reasons.

Dave Zien
Million Mile Motorcycle Rider/Former
Wisconsin State Senator
Eau Claire, Wisconsin

On March 2nd, 2010, Dave Zien rode to his 130th World Record when he completed riding 135,037 miles in one year. Wow! But wait, there's more!

Here's another – even more impressive achievement: In April 2009, he earned a World Record from the Iron Butt Association for riding one million miles on the same motorcycle - his 1991 Harley Davidson FXRT. You can see that record-setting million mile bike in the Sturgis Motorcycle Museum and Hall of Fame. Harley-Davidson recognized the milestone by presenting him with a new motorcycle.

Zien enjoyed his celebrity status as he visited with many close friends during the Sturgis Rally. As is his custom, he pressed a lot of flesh with old friends, current supporters, and new fans.

Faces

Chapter Six

Camping & Entertainment

Roughing it in Sturgis

The word camping means different things to different people, and this fact is especially true in Sturgis. For some, it means a tent and sleeping bag strapped to the sissy bar or stuffed in the saddle bags. Others see camping as an opportunity to limber up the RV, complete with air conditioning and an enclosed trailer for bikes. In light of the variation in camping styles, most of the big campgrounds in and near Sturgis now offer space for tents, as well as hook ups for RVs.

No matter how they define camping, most people at the Sturgis rally like the idea of camping alongside their bikes. There's only one problem - picking a place that fits your idea of a good time. There are dozens of facilities that cater to Rally goers. Some are huge – thousands of acres – while others are quiet, getaway spots in more remote locations.

A survey of the Sturgis and South Dakota tourist literature lists descriptions like convenient locations, terrific views, laundry services, wi-fi, general merchandise stores, showers, handicap access, ATV rentals, shady camp spots, electrical hookups, food vendors, restaurants, beer gardens, bars and bike wash stations. A few even have shuttle bus service into Sturgis.

The big facilities in and near Sturgis – the focus of this chapter – have definitely seen the move to bigger and better everything in the last few years. A good example might be swimming pools, which now seem standard at many of the big party-grounds. And by swimming pools we don't mean the little kidney shaped pools located in the parking lot of the mom and pop motels that date to the days of Ozzie and Harriet. No, we mean acres of pure blue water contained by concrete and surrounded by more acres of decks and, yes, the mandatory bar. If you want your water hot and frothy instead of cool and calm, just jump into one of the available hot tubs. No pool party is complete without music, and at least one of the party pools includes its own bandstand with live music every afternoon.

Big pools are just one example of the bigger is better phenomena going on in Sturgis. The majority of the better-known "campgrounds" have morphed into small cities, with populations big-ger than many real towns. By the time you consider the long list of available services, from showers to food, bike repair to entertainment, there is very little reason to leave the small city of your choice. And if you do decide to head Downtown, most of these facilities offer the already mentioned bus rides.

Like all things - camping in Sturgis has changed. Back in the day we slept on the ground, with or without a tent. You can still sleep on the ground, but if you'd rather sleep in an RV, or a cabin, or the small trailer you towed behind the bike, all these options are available – as are a long list of service and entertainment options for the hours when you aren't sleeping.

Here's a sampling of other campground/RV sites:
- American Pines Vacation Homes
- Badlands Ranch & Resort
- Bear Butte Creek Campground
- Beaver Lake Campground
- BernieVille Rally Campground
- Broken Boot Campground
- Broken Spoke Campground
- The Buffalo Chip Campground
- Bulldog Campground
- Centennial Campground
- Chris' Campground
- Cottonwood Creek Camp
- CreekSide CampGround
- Elk Creek Resort & Lodge
- Jo's Field of Dreams Campground
- Glencoe CampResort
- Hog Heaven Campground
- Iron Horse Campground
- Katmandu Campground
- Lamphere Ranch Campground
- Free Spirit Campground
- No Name City Campground
- Shade Valley Campground
- Recreational Springs
- Ride 'N' Rest Campground
- Rush No More Campground
- Spokane Creek Resort, Keystone
- Sturgis Road Campground
- Sturgis View Campground
- Suzie's Camp
- Tatanka Hill
- Tilford Gulch Campground

Broken Spoke

Nestled up against the pristine foothills of gorgeous Bear Butte outside Sturgis, The Broken Spoke was the place to be for wall-to-wall entertainment during the 70th Annual Sturgis Motorcycle Rally.

You couldn't go wrong just kicking back and enjoying the sights, sounds, action, and people watching just about anywhere on the 660-acre Broken Spoke grounds. There was more than plenty to do, like swimming in the World's Biggest Biker Pool (with hot tubs & Tiki Bar), Legends Art Gallery, Good 'ol Days Raceway, Hill Climb, America's Original Extreme Motorcycle Thrill Shows, the Limpnickie Lot (where attendees interacted with the next generation of bike builders), the Lucky Daredevil thrill show, outrageous con-tests, free shuttle from the campground to the Broken Spoke Saloon in downtown Sturgis, live music at several bars, and an on-site General Store.

Other events during the week included the IMBBA Bike Show and Hall of Fame Awards, Easyriders Rodeo, the Michael Lichter & Sugar Bear Ride, Cycle Source Ride and Chopper Show, Vietnam Veterans Tribute Wall "The Wall that Heals," Baker Drivetrain Smoke-Down Showdown, and the S&S Smokeout. As the exit sign says: "Till next time - Keep the shiny side up and the rubber side down!"

And don't forget the music! Check out these headliners who rocked the crowd at the Broken Spoke:

.38 Special • Eddie Money • Black Oak Arkansas • Warrant • Great White • Dokken • Gallagher • Black Stone Cherry • Confederate Railroad • Kentucky Headhunters

Buffalo Chip

The legendary Buffalo Chip has time and again proven itself as the epicenter of Sturgis Bike Week and with Rally Week celebrating its 70th Anniversary, this year was no exception.

One of the quirkiest additions to the Chip's 2010 Rally lineup was Pee-wee Herman, hot on the comeback trail with a Broadway show scheduled for fall 2010. Pee-wee helped kick off this year's 70th Annual Sturgis Rally Week 2010.

Besides great music, there were other artistic offerings. Famed photographer Michael Lichter's 10th Annual Motorcycles as Art exhibit, "Eternal Combustion-30 in the Wind," focused on the explosion of interest and passion for custom motorcycles and featured the works of 15 pairs of custom builders. Adorning the walls of the exhibit was a collection of his images from his archive of limited edition prints, including some never before seen.

Then there was even more biker-centric entertainment and fun available. The Guns of Freedom gave guests the opportunity to fire over 65 models of machine guns; the Freedom Celebration included The American Pride RideT and a special tribute to our American Veterans and Active Duty Military. There was the ABATE Rodeo, the Miss Buffalo Chip Pageant, the South Dakota Mud Races, the 2K10 Challenge, a Demoltion Derby, Burnout Drags Competition and a Pink & Proud Reception. Whew! Now you know why they call it the Best Party Anywhere!

Now that the 2010 party is over, watch out because next year the Buffalo Chip is sure to be going ALL OUT for its 30th anniversary in 2011.

Entertainment is front and center at the Chip. Guests got close and personal with a genuine selection of premier bands and musical superstars, including:

Tesla • Drowning Pool • Motley Crue • Creedence Clearwater Revisited • The Guess Who • Trailer Choir • Buckcherry • ZZ Top • Bob Dylan • Orianthi • Stonesour • Motley Crue • Jason Aldean • Ozzy Osbourne • Disturbed • The Scorpions • Williams & Ree • The Doobie Brothers • Dave Mason • Lee Rocker

Glencoe

Any discussion of major campgrounds with entertainment would have to include Glencoe. One of the first of the truly big campgrounds in Sturgis, Glencoe CampResort has been the home away from home for tens of thousands of Sturgis Rally patrons for over 20 years. As the Sturgis Rally has grown, so has this family-owned and operated facility, just three miles outside Sturgis. Glencoe has seen many expansions and upgrades including the purchase of additional shaded acreage for camping, and the planting of hundreds of new trees. Other improvements to the grounds and the facilities include more paved roads to help reduce dust, new and improved bathrooms, as well as bigger and better shower houses with abundant hot water.

Glencoe is currently over 600 acres and boasts about 1,000 RV sites, and offers campers a full-service convenience store, shopping and entertainment. And let's not forget that it's the site of the infamous Titty Alley, the main road through the campground where after dark you can see a steady stream of motorcycles, golf carts, four-wheelers and trailers hauling men and women in various stages of undress. Imagine Mardi Gras in the Great Outdoors.

Glencoe Camp Resort has the largest outdoor amphitheater (Rock N' The Rally) in the country with room for over 125,000 people. Past acts have been Kiss, Kenney Chesney, Steve Miller Band, Ted Nugent, Nickelback, Sammy Hagar, Godsmack, Big N Rich, .38 Special and many others.

The Glencoe Campground and Glencoe Pavillion boast some of the best entertainment of the entire Sturgis Rally. From Strugis House Bands to Concerts from Creed, Godsmack and More.

Full Throttle

If you were one of the estimated 30,000 people per day who checked out the scene at the Full Throttle Saloon during the 2010 Rally, you just might see yourself on TruTV.

The packed schedule of events and activities for its customers, combined with a behind-the scenes look at real-time operational logistics during the hectic Rally season, created the perfect backdrop for Full Throttle's TruTV documentary series. A crew of 45 was on location working on the series that aired during the fall 2010 season.

And those cameras had plenty to do, since the fun never let up.

For starters, there was the 11th annual Bikers Ball with a FTS Tattoo Contest and a Salute to Our Troops. Other activities included Angieland, Midget Wrestling , Paul Yaffe's Bagger Nation Bike Show, FTS Zip Line, Rhett Rotten Wall of Death, Pappy Hoel Memorial Ride, Human Sling Shot, Beer Belly Contest, Burnout Pit, Mechanical Bull, GFTS Biker Olympics and (I love this one) "99 Beautiful Bartenders and ONE Ugly One!"

"The Full Throttle is the number one blue collar biker bar in the United States," according to a posting by owner Michael Ballard on his website. "Everyone is welcome, but it's well known that factory workers, construction workers and any kind of guy who busts his ass and saves his money all year is gonna be welcome at the Throttle."

The Full Throttle evening concerts featured these headliners:

Brother Clyde featuring Billy Ray Cyrus • Bret Michaels • Marshall Tucker Band • Jackyl • Ice T

Chapter Seven

Biker Chicks

Beauty amid the Beasts

Kimmy Cruz

Kimmy Cruz
Traveling Celebrity & Bartender
Bryant, Arkansas

It doesn't take long to get to know Kimmy Cruz. The self-described "Angel of Fire" is a promoter, model, photographer and bartender and a true force of nature in the biker community. With her lovely, southern-tinged accent she explained "I've been on the major rally circuit for years. This year I will do 20 shows like Sturgis, Daytona Bike Week, Laconia, Arizona Bike Week, Bike Blues & BBQ, and the Republic of Texas

Rally. I love it!"

This is her tenth appearance at Sturgis and this year she's working at the Firehouse Saloon for three weeks. Dressed in hot biker chic regalia, she efficiently runs the bar, but often stops what's she doing to accommodate photo opp requests from customers, old friends and new fans.

"I was a hairdresser by trade. To do that, and this kind of work, you have to be a people person in order to enjoy what you're doing," she explained. "Someday soon though I want to show off my photography skills with an exhibit during a rally."

It's sometimes best to let a good promoter do what they do best. In this case, describe herself. As she explains on her website bio: "I've been intensely involved in the motorcycle industry for more than 10 years -- from Dennis Kirk product representation at Easyriders Shows to Samson Exhaust product representation at 2010 Expos. From my start as a sales rep for Thunder Roads in 2002 and The Ride Magazine in 2004, I began traveling all over the U.S.A. covering anything and everything that has to do with two wheels. Rallies, Poker Runs, Bike Events, Motorcycle Shows, Motocross, Biker Weddings, Toy Runs, Club House Coverage, you name it - I have covered it."

Tatania Elias

Tatania Elias
Server, Temporary Insanity
Scottsdale, Arizona

Tatania and her closest girlfriends work as servers at Ra Sushi restaurants in metro Phoenix, Arizona. A few weeks before the Sturgis rally, one of those ladies met a gentleman while working in the Scottsdale restaurant who asked her if she would be interested in working a 10-day server gig at his restaurant in Sturgis, Temporary Insanity, during the rally. The girls talked it up between themselves for a few days. They had a feel for the biker crowd since one of the Ra Sushi locations they worked on a regular basis was close to the famous Billet Bar in Scottsdale. "It looked like an interesting group of folks," she said. That one young lady gathered up three of her friends, including Tatania, an off they went to Sturgis. "It sounded like fun – seeing that part of the country, making some

good money, and having some adventures," Tatania said. Since Temporary Insanity is located right on Main Street in Sturgis, they definitely had their hands full every day. She admitted the shifts were long, but not exactly unexpected. The group of Arizona gals still found time to get the experiences they were seeking. Of course they explored the downtown Sturgis scene, then made lots of new friends with bikers and non bikers from all over the country, and were even offered a ride to Mt. Rushmore by three Hells Angels. "It was only my second time on a bike. That will definitely be a trip I remember for the rest of my life, that's for sure," Tatania said. "It was really great. Those guys were sweet."

Gloria Struck

Gloria Struck
Female Riding Legend
Clifton, New Jersey

Here's how one reporter described Gloria Struck: "The spunky 84-year-old woman stands a tad over five feet tall and can't weigh more than a buck five. But she has the heart of a lion. "

Talk with Gloria for a while and you definitely sense the powerful spirit behind the way she has lived her life. In the process, she has become a riding legend and icon in the biker community.

These days her rides are fewer in number (but longer in mileage) and dependent on her daughter's work schedule. Notwithstanding some restrictions, in 2009 she logged 3,775 miles riding her 2004 Harley Softtail Classic to gatherings in places like Cody, WY and Daytona Beach, FL.

She is a much-honored member of the Motor Maids Inc., the first and oldest continuously operated women's motorcycling organization in North America. Founded in 1940 they claim 1,200 members across the US and Canada. As an organization, the Motor Maids were inducted into the Sturgis Hall of Fame in 2005 with the J.C. "Pappy" Hoel Outstanding Achievement Award.

Gloria has been an active member for 64 years! She and fellow Motor Maid Betty Fauls were the first to get 60-year member cards from the famed group. Next year they get their 65 year card.

"Lots of people call me an inspiration," she commented. "Well, I always have plans, something to look forward to. When I was 25 year old, I always wanted to ride in Europe. And at age 74, I finally did it with my son. You have to live your dreams!"

Gloria Struck is still leading a remarkable life. As she shares one of her many amazing stories, you can only imagine all the places she's seen, the different people she's met, and the on-the-road experiences she's had throughout decades traveling across the changing cultural landscape of America.

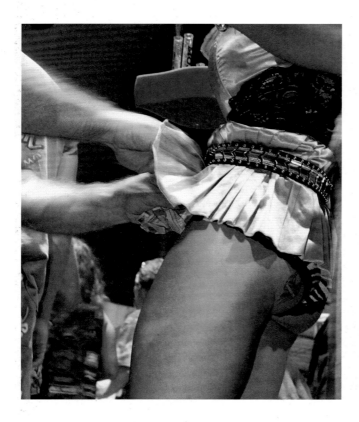

Chapter Eight

Get Out and Ride

Get Outa Downtown

People who've never been to Sturgis assume we spend all of our time on Main Street, or at one of the big campgrounds they've heard so much about. And sadly, for some riders, especially newbies, that's what happens. They arrive, they hang out, they hang out some more, then they head home. To say they're missing the boat is a gross understatement, because there is simply so much more to see. From Mount Rushmore to Alzada, Montana, there are more places to go and more two lane roads connecting all those places than anyone can imagine.

In putting together this chapter we kind of cherry-picked the list of possible destinations. We've left out some of the really easy ones, like Rushmore - though we did leave Spearfish Canyon in the mix, thinking that there are a few riders who haven't seen Bridal Veil Falls, or enjoyed breakfast at the Latchstring.

The idea is to get you out of Downtown, out of your old standard haunts, and on the road. Get up early, don't dawdle and don't let that little hangover (from hanging out in the motel parking lot 'till two AM) get in the way. Get out and go. Many of the spots mentioned, and other good ones have been discovered by other riders. Which is not to say they aren't worth the ride. It does mean however, that in most cases you won't have the place, or the road, all to yourself unless you get going early.

Along the way you're likely to make a few discoveries of your own. Maybe one of the riders in your group needs to make a nature stop in some little joint along the way, and it turns into a two hour break. Hey, that's the whole idea, because even the South Dakota guide books don't list all the neat little towns, or scenic roads, or historic stops.

The best thing about the small towns and the beer tent behind the gas station is the people you meet while you're there. The folks in Sturgis are nice, but some of them get a little burned out. In Rochford or Sundance, however, they really look forward to the bikers, and not just for our money. Take a minute to talk with the rancher or the cowboy at the bar, they all have a story to tell and they're likely anxious to hear yours as well.

Rochford, SD

Rochford is where you end up if you happen to be riding from Deadwood or Lead, headed toward Cheyenne Crossing, and get lost on a two lane that runs south with no apparent destination. Just keep riding, because at the end of Hwy. 205 is a neat little town that's a throwback to simpler days. To the days before Walmart, Starbucks, and Malls filled with stuff we don't really need.

What Rochford does have is a nice bar and restaurant with a big porch on the front with some old beat up chairs. So get yourself a cup of coffee or a cool one, and sit back to consider what it must be like to live here when it's not Rally Week.

Alzada, MT

T-Shirts from The Stoneville Saloon in Alzada say, "Conveniently located in the middle of nowhere." According to Diane, owner of Stoneville, the reality is, "we're on the way to everywhere," including Hulett, Devils Tower and Belle Fourche. Friends I know run to Alzada every year, and they make it a loop, riding up Hwy 112 from Hulett, then back to Spearfish and Sturgis via Hwy 212. "Rally is the best time of year for us" explains Diane. "We have homemade chili, burgers, and pulled pork sandwiches. This year I started 'topless Tuesday' and it went over so well I'm doing it every year from now on."

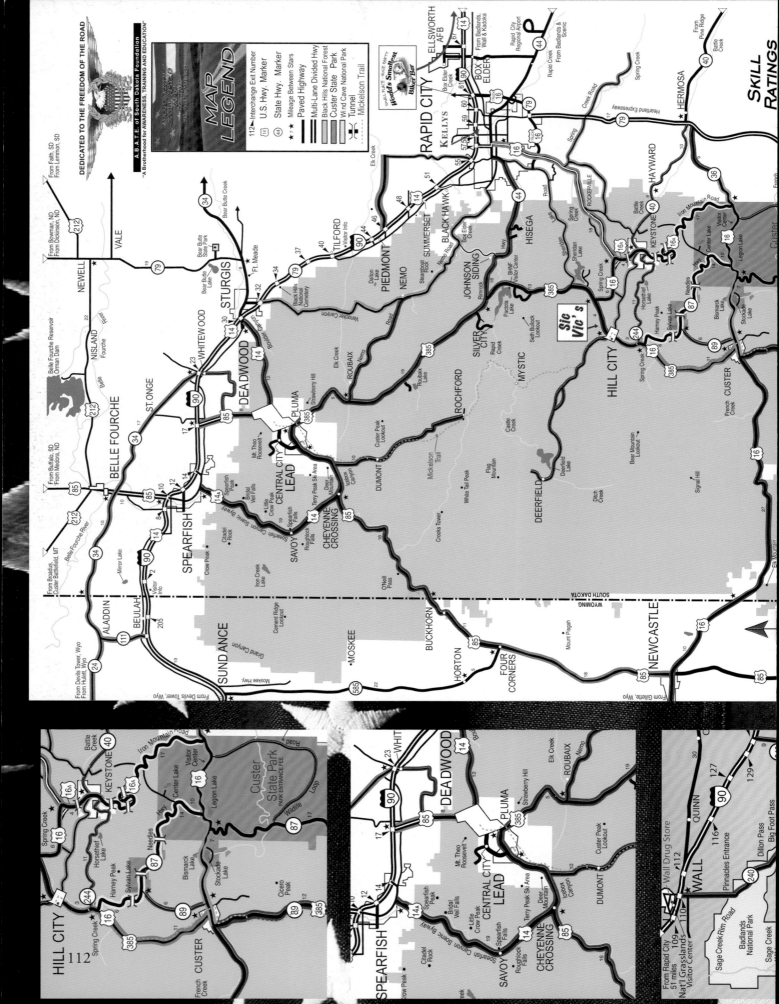

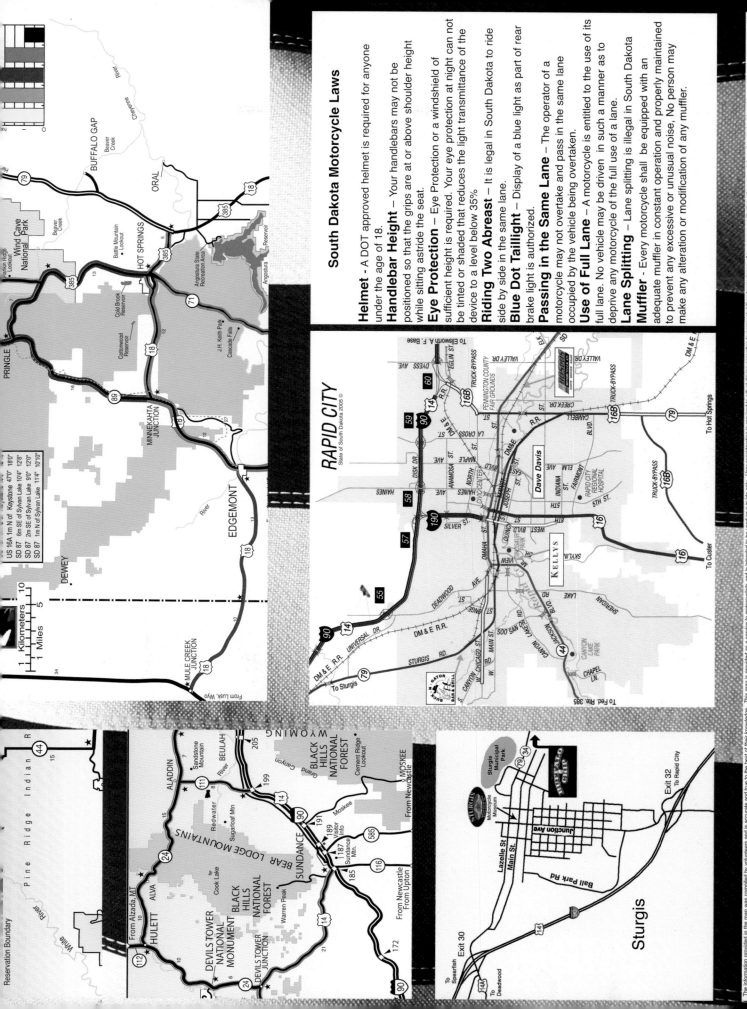

South Dakota Motorcycle Laws

Helmet – A DOT approved helmet is required for anyone under the age of 18.

Handlebar Height – Your handlebars may not be positioned so that the grips are at or above shoulder height while sitting astride the seat.

Eye Protection – Eye Protection or a windshield of sufficient height is required. Your eye protection at night can not be tinted or shaded that reduces the light transmittance of the device to a level below 35%

Riding Two Abreast – It is legal in South Dakota to ride side by side in the same lane.

Blue Dot Taillight – Display of a blue light as part of rear brake light is authorized.

Passing in the Same Lane – The operator of a motorcycle may not overtake and pass in the same lane occupied by the vehicle being overtaken.

Use of Full Lane – A motorcycle is entitled to the use of its full lane. No vehicle may be driven in such a manner as to deprive any motorcycle of the full use of a lane.

Lane Splitting – Lane splitting is illegal in South Dakota

Muffler - Every motorcycle shall be equipped with an adequate muffler in constant operation and properly maintained to prevent any excessive or unusual noise, No person may make any alteration or modification of any muffler.

US 16A 1m N of Keystone 47°0' 180'
SD 87 6m SE of Sylvan Lake 104° 128'
SD 87 2m SE of Sylvan Lake 90° 120'
SD 87 1m N of Sylvan Lake 114° 10'10'

RAPID CITY
State of South Dakota 2005 ©

Reservation Boundary

Sturgis

The information provided in the map was compiled by volunteers and is accurate and true to the best of their knowledge. This map is provided as a service to motorcyclists and is intended to be used as a guide only. User consideration is required to adjust driving according to personal skill and experience. Any person or entity that relies on any information obtained from this map does so at their own risk. All information on this map is provided "As Is" without warranties or conditions, expressed or implied, including, but not limited to, warranties for product quality, or suitability to a particular purpose or use. The risk and or liability resulting from the use of this map is assumed entirely by the user. All entities involved with the information provided on this map share no liability with the users in any direct, indirect, incidental, special, or consequential damages whatsoever, including, but not limited to loss of revenue, lost or damaged property, or economic loss, or any loss due to bodily injury or death.

Faces

Photos by Colleen Swartz

Faces

Spearfish Canyon, SD

I'm thinking the road to heaven looks a lot like Spearfish Canyon - not that most of us will ever know for sure. It's been discovered, but that doesn't mean it isn't worth a run early in the morning. Start out in Spearfish, ride the canyon to Latchstring. Stop for breakfast, and then continue on to Cheyenne Crossing. At the crossing you can either turn left for Rochford or Deadwood; or take the road less traveled. So turn right, and leave the traffic behind. Keep on rolling as the canyon levels out and the forested shoulders roll you to Buckhorn, where they hand out condoms with the label, "keeping our customers safe."

Deadwood, SD

The best thing about the gambling in Deadwood - isn't the gambling. It's the fact that a percentage of the profits go to building restoration and maintenance. Which is why the Franklin Hotel and the Bodega are in such good condition.

Whether you like to gamble or not - take a ride up the mountain, either up Bolder Canyon Highway from Sturgis, or Hwy. 85 from the freeway. Either way the vistas are great and the traffic never gets too bad. For people watching, check out the veranda at the Franklin, or the upper deck of the Stockade. And ya gotta have at least one beer, and maybe get a T-shirt at the Number 10 Saloon.

Wyoming

The black hills might be grand and breathtaking, but the mixed prairie of Wyoming - just a little farther west - is equally beautiful, though in a more subtle fashion.

Start with refreshments at The Dime in Sundance and make the loop to Devils Tower, Hulett, Aladdin and Stone House Saloon. The only thing better than sitting at the Stone House taking pictures of friends, is coming over a rise on the way there, only to see the thin ribbon of asphalt unwind ahead of you, while the sound of six or eight bikes running down the road fills your ears with motorcycle music.

Devils Tower, SD

The first couple of times you see Devil's Tower you wonder, "what the hell is that big rock doing standing all by itself in the middle of the prairie?" It turns out Devils Tower is the core of an old, old volcano. As cool as the tower is, the best thing about the tower is the getting there. Most people take the freeway part way, and then turn off on Hwy. 14 or 111 to go north. An equally good route is to run farther west to exit #154, then come at Devils Tower from the southwest. Either way, riding to the Tower means many miles of two lanes roads, and scenery that varies from prairie to forest.

Chapter Nine

Music

From Bob Dylan to Kid Rock

There's more than just riding and partyin' to do in Sturgis – there's music. Man, is there music. Every little bar and many of the campgrounds have a band of some kind. It might be a one-man band, like the cowboy who plays every year at the Stockade in Deadwood, or a little three-piece group similar to the one I heard in one of the bars in Hulett, WY. In addition to the small bars and small bands, there is true name entertainment of the highest caliber every night at a number of different locations.

To list the bands available all week reads like a who's who of rock n roll. The Buffalo Chip, one of the first campgrounds to bring in top-name entertainment, offered up: Motley Crue, Scorpions, Tesla, Kid Rock, ZZ Top, Jason Aldean, Doobie Brothers, Buckcherry, Dave Mason, The Guess Who, Creedence Clearwater Revisited, Trailer Choir, Drowning Pool. Williams & Ree, and Ross & Rottten.

Monkey Rock, countered with Godsmack, Alice in Chains, Creed, Stone Temple Pilots, 3 Doors Down, Three Days Grace, Hinder, Wolfmother, Skillet, Hellyeah and Eagles of Death Metal. Just a little farther north, the Broken Spoke gave riders a chance to see Blackfoot, .38 Special, Great White, Black Oak Arkansas, Eddie Money, the comedian Gallagher, Confederate Railroad, Warrant, and Black Stone Cherry. And we haven't talked about Full Throttle or Glencoe or…

As noted, the first rate "music" included comedians and performers like Gallagher. With a wall of plastic behind him, necessitated by what happens during the later part of the show, Gallagher starts with a monologue that pretty much insults and derides every political party, group, religion, and association. Only after he's verbally assaulted pretty much everyone in the audience, does he move on to part two. Imagine this: one table, one oversized can of cream style corn, one insane person armed with an oversized hammer. Now imagine what happens when the insane man brings the hammer down – onto the corn container, which happens to be aimed at the crowd.

It's all in good fun. And good fun and great music is what thousands and thousands of riders and enthusiasts enjoy every year. More than just the epicenter of motorcycling, Sturgis has become - for one week each year – the center of high quality music and entertainment.

122

"Legends never die, they live on in our hearts and minds forever"

Chapter Ten

Sturgis by the Numbers

How Many: People, Tickets, Toilets, Beers...

Attendance: While difficult to accurately measure, Rally officials estimate that at least 600,000 people attended this year's 70th anniversary rally. In 2009, attendance was estimated at just under 450,000.

Traffic Jams: The South Dakota Department of Transportation estimates 460,000 vehicles entered Sturgis during Rally week from August 9-15. That's up 17.2% from 2009.

Adding in traffic counts from the days leading up to the rally brings the total to 600,000 vehicles, which is what local officials had expected.

Riding for a Cause: Hamsters USA and the Legends Riders raised $52,000 this year on their 50 mile Legends Ride. The funds were split by the Sky Ranch for Boys and the Sturgis Motorcycle Hall of Fame and Museum. The annual event has raised $150,000 for charity since it was started three years ago.

Only "The Man" Knows: The exact number of law enforcement agents who work the Rally is a well kept secret.

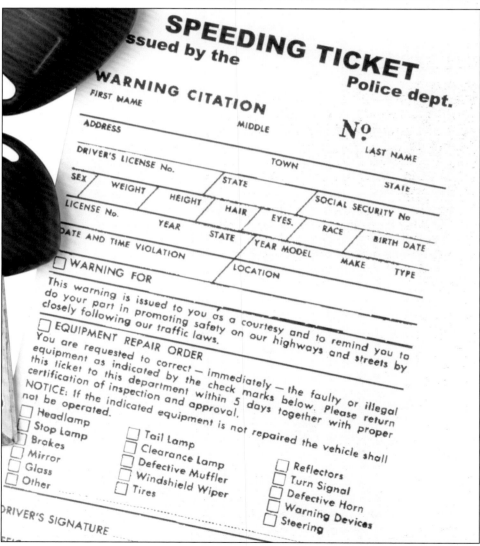

Riding Tragedy: The official death tally for the 2010 rally hit nine, a significant jump over a fatality-free 2009 rally.

Rally Connected Deaths: At least 12 other motorcyclist deaths that occurred elsewhere in South Dakota and surrounding states were attributed to the rally

DUIs Down: DUI arrests were down when compared to 2009. The Highway Patrol reported 290 DUI arrests. In 2009, 316 drivers were ticketed for DUI in the Black Hills.

Don't Litter Dept: In a typical week, Sturgis residents generate an average of 24 tons of trash, but during rally week that figure shoots up to 63 tons.

Know your National Monuments: Mount Rushmore officials say 17,600 people visited the national memorial on Tuesday August 17 during Rally Week . That's the most in one day since the park started keeping track in 2000.

Best Rides Outside Sturgis City Limits: Mount Rushmore (62 miles), Crazy Horse Memorial (67 miles), Custer State Park (75 miles), Spearfish Canyon (20 miles), Deadwood (13 miles) and the Badlands (110 miles).

Been there, done that, got the T-shirt: The South Dakota Department of Revenue and Regulation reported that sales and tourism tax revenues collected from temporary vendors at this year's Rally totaled $989,911 in the Northern Hills, which includes Sturgis and all other communities in Meade and Lawrence counties. Those revenues were up $127,804 from last year's total of $862,107.

Of the $989,911 collected, $545,824 was state sales tax, $232,328 was municipal sales tax, $8,196 was municipal gross receipts tax, and $203,563 was state tourism tax revenue.

There were 1,207 vendors displaying and selling products at the 2010 Rally, compared to 1,149 in 2009 and 1,191 in 2008. Gross vendor sales totaled $13,647,413 this year in the Northern Hills area – an increase of $1,728,798 from last year's gross sales of $11,918,615.

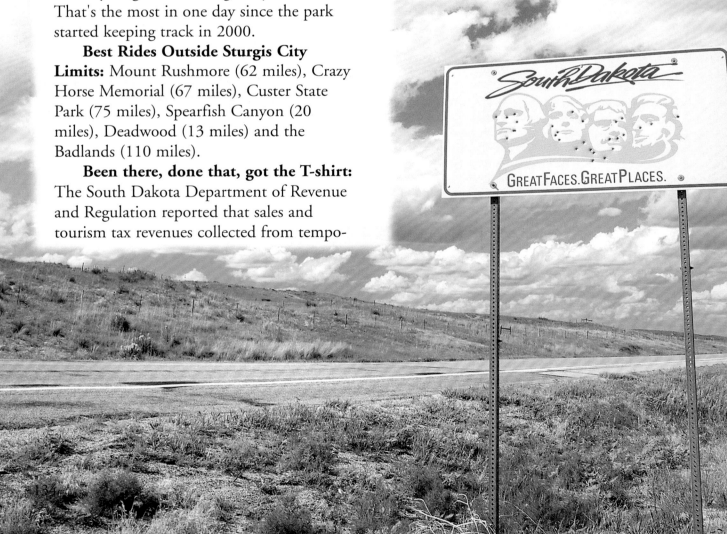

Bikers Behaving Badly

**Sturgis Police Department
Rally Report 2010**

Injury accidents - 8

Non-injury accidents - 21

Fight calls/disturbances/assault - 31
Burglary/theft - 19

Misdemeanor drug/paraphernalia
possession - 51

Felony drug possession - 7

Assault - 2

Driving While Intoxicated - 23

Open container in vehicle - 41

Illegal parking - 130

Tickets issued - 366

Charges to locals (defined as those who are
from West River in South Dakota and eastern
Wyoming) -- 99

**S.D. Highway Patrol
Rally Report 2010**
*(Numbers cover Sturgis, Lawrence County,
Rapid City, Southern Hills and the Badlands
areas)*

DUI -- 290
(Last year to date -316)

Misdemeanor Drug arrests - 183
(Last year to date -- 153)

Felony drug arrests - 46
(Last year to date - 43)

Other felony arrests - 2
(Last year to date - 3)

Total citations - 1,442
(Last year to date -1,803)

Total warnings - 4,598
(Last year to date -4,363)

Non-injury accidents - 36
(Last year to date - 39)

Injury accidents - 73
(Last year to date - 72)

Fatal accidents - 9
(Last year to date - 0)

Chapter Eleven

Survival

Travel, Trouble & Legal Advice

The Souvenirs You Take Home

Like a moth to a flame, Sturgis draws us from every state in the union to a nondescript little town in western South Dakota. And like the moth, once there, we just can't get enough. We bump up against the brightest lights again and again, no matter that it might hurt when we do. In fact, there are so many lights screaming for our attention that it's hard to know which to pick. Party with friends? Ride to Wyoming and party with new friends? Ride the back roads at high speed? Maybe it's time to line up for a turn in the burnout pit? Or just hang out in any of the big campgrounds listening to music?

Electricity is in the air - if you can't feel it, if you don't sense the temptation on the street - call 911 because you must be dead. The trick for most of us is to eat lightly from the buffet, to have a great time without running afoul of the law, and without accident or incident on the motorcycle.

The By the Numbers chart in Chapter 10 is a good place to start when considering Things to Avoid; DUI rates at the top of the list. There are more cops per square inch in and around Sturgis than you can imagine. On the second Friday of the week I drove from one of the campgrounds out on Hwy 79, back to Whitewood, and the radar detector lit up about every hundred yards. This is not to mention the foot patrols and cruisers in Sturgis proper, or the cop car sitting in a dark parking lot along the main street as I came into Whitewood.

The odds are stacked against you. So the trick – though it sounds too obvious to state – is to do your heavy drinking (or whatever) later in the day after you've made it back to the motel or campground. There is nothing better than a couple of cool ones after a ride to Sundance or Deadwood, but remember that driving down the mountain late in the afternoon on Highway 85 is like running the gauntlet, and it can be a long trip from Sundance to Sturgis. And before you assume that any tickets you get in Sturgis "stay in Sturgis," think again. That is a myth, or at least not something you want to count on, as a friend of mine found out when his reckless driving ticket did indeed show up on his record back in his home state.

Though not specifically spelled out in The Numbers, there are a couple of additional Situations to Avoid. The first, once again, is alcohol related. Don't assume you can walk out of a bar onto the busy street outside with a beer in your hands. Sometimes you can and sometimes you can't, and if you mix the two up it's an easy way to start a conversation with one of the boys in blue. Public nudity is another good way to start one of those conversations. If you're going to pop the top, be sure you're on private property, or at least NOT standing in the middle of the street in downtown Sturgis. The same applies to taking a pee between two cars in the parking lot 'cause it's too far to walk to the port-a-potties. Better to walk a block than get a free sleeping room in the courthouse.

Which is not to preach doom and gloom or Just Say No. For a motorcycle nut, Sturgis is more fun that just about any place on earth. If you're not having too much fun most of the time, then you're doing something wrong. Just be sure the only souvenirs you bring home are T shirts and photographs.

South Dakota Motorcycle Laws 101

Make a point to get a copy of the "Motorcycle Skill Rated Map of the Black Hills" for current, accurate information, riding tips and road conditions in and around Sturgis. The map is produced through a joint venture between A.B.A.T.E. of South Dakota Foundation and the Office of Highway Safety. Here's their list of applicable South Dakota Motorcycle Laws:

Helmet – A DOT approved helmet is required for anyone under the age of 18.

Handlebar Height – Your handlebars may not be positioned so that the grips are at or above shoulder height while sitting astride the seat.

Eye Protection – Eye Protection or a windshield of sufficient height is required. Your eye protection at night can not be tinted or shaded that reduces the light transmittance of the device to a level below 35%.

Riding Two Abreast – It is legal in South Dakota to ride side by side in the same lane.

Blue Dot Taillight – Display of a blue light as part of rear break light is authorized.

Passing in the Same Lane – The operator of a motorcycle may not overtake and pass in the same lane occupied by the vehicle being overtaken.

Use of Full Lane – A motorcycle is entitled to the use of its full lane. No vehicle may be driven in such a manner as to deprive any motorcycle of the full use of a lane.

Lane Splitting – Lane splitting is illegal in South Dakota.

Muffler – Every motorcycle shall be equipped with an adequate muffler in constant operation and properly maintained to prevent any excessive or unusual noise. No person may make any alteration or modification of any muffler.

For more information, visit www.abatesd.com

On the Road to Sturgis
August 8-14, 2011

So, are you ready for YOUR Sturgis experience? If you're coming back, or even if you're a newbie, here's some inside scoop as you plan on making the scene in 2011. Start here:

The Official Sturgis Rally Website:
www.sturgismotorcyclerally.com

South Dakota Office of Tourism:
www.travelsd.com
800-SDakota

City of Sturgis:
www.sturgis-sd.gov
605-720-0800

Sturgis Chamber of Commerce/Visitor Information:
http://www.sturgis-sd.org/

Sturgis Rally on Facebook:
http://www.facebook.com/sturgisrally

Area Map:
http://www.springhillpressmaps.com/us/southdakota/rapidcity/

How to get there? Ride your bike, duh! Or, you can fly into the closest airport in Rapid City, SD.

Where to stay? Not a problem. There's something for everyone and every budget - - lush private house rentals, group lodges, motels designed for bikers, casino/hotels in Deadwood, RV parks, chain hotels, campgrounds, bed & breakfasts, you name it. No matter where you stay, be prepared to pay a premium. After all, this is how the locals make money during their high season.

While the action is centered in downtown Sturgis, you won't go wrong checking out or booking accommodations in any of these locales throughout the surrounding area:

Badlands	Keystone	Rapid City
Custer	Lead	Spearfish
Deadwood	Murdo	Sturgis
Edgemont	Nemo	Wall
Hill City	Philip	Whitewood
Hot Springs	Piedmont	

See you in 2011. Last one in buys the beer!

Sugar Bear Lovold

Sugar Bear Lovold
Business Owner
Sturgis, South Dakota

In the mid-seventies, Sugar Bear Lovold and partner Paul Ullreich worked driving trucks in and around the Dakotas. They covered a lot of ground throughout the surrounding states too, but felt a special pull towards Sturgis - the country, the people, the overall vibe of the place. It was there they set up Sturgis Tattoo and catered to the locals, year-round tourists and, of course, the Rally crowd. Since 1990 they've been in the same location - just a block off Main Street - and feel like they've grown along with the Rally. "I think people love coming back to Sturgis each year for a chance to see what's new. Clothes, bike parts, motorcycles, all kinds of new products. So, every year we try to add something new, something different. Our big sellers are Sturgis Rally year tattoos, Deadwood and Native American designs. We do custom work, whatever the customer wants," he added.

Besides Sturgis Tattoo, the long-time partners operate two other businesses in Sturgis, both located on Main Street - Road Kill Café and Main Street Tattoos. What's it like to run three businesses this time of year? Sugar Bear thought for a moment and answered "It's a lot of work, but it's a lot of fun too. Every year is like a reunion. It's great to see everybody."

Rhonda Vance and Cactus Jack

Rhonda Vance and Cactus Jack
Hat Sellers
Colorado Springs, Colorado

Cactus Jack and Rhonda Vance know hats – and the open road. For 22 years they've been setting up shop 51 times a year around the country at special shows, festivals and rallys. Even though they offer all styles of headwear, their specialty is Panama Leaf Hats from Guatemala. "These are the original Panama hats. Good to wear for any occasion," explained Cactus Jack.

While only his second year at Sturgis, and from his sales booth on the Buffalo Chip grounds, he sensed that the crowd was bigger this year. Being outside all day long, he appreciated that the weather held up, too. "We love the great folks here, the entertainment, the atmosphere," he said. "We're having a great time."

Their next stop is Tulsa, Oklahoma. If you miss them there, keep an eye out at the next Rally, fair or festival you attend. There's a darned good chance you'll run into Cactus Jack and Rhonda. Be sure to say "Hi" to these folks – and buy a hat!

Sources

Buffalo Chip
www.buffalochip.com

Broken Spoke
www.brokenspokecampground.com

Glencoe
www.glencoecamp.com

Full Throttle
www.fullthrottlesaloon.com
Full Throttle can also be found
on Tru TV

Scooter Grubb
Emperor of Images
scootershoots@gmail.com

Maverick Publishing
www.americanbagger.com

South Dakota DOT
www.sddot.com
Good source or travel information,
including highway construction projects.

More Great Books From Wolfgang Publications!
http://www.wolfpub.com

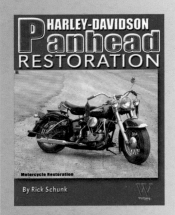

HARLEY-DAVIDSON PANHEAD RESTORATION

Among all the older Harley-Davidson models, none holds the allure of the Panhead. The bike some would call the first modern Harley. Well-known author Rick Schunk starts the discussion of Panheads with a brief history lesson, followed by a list of things to look for, and avoid, when shopping for a Panhead.

The engine and transmission are two major components sure to require attention during the restoration or repair of your Panhead. Rick documents the overhaul of both an engine and a transmission with two extensive photo sequences.

While there are other restoration guides, there are no how-to restoration books that provide extensive, start-to-finish photo sequences explaining each major operation necessary to the restoration of a Harley-Davidson Panhead.

| Ten Chapters | 176 Pages | $34.95 | Over 500 photos, 100% color |

HOW TO BUILD A CHEAP CHOPPER

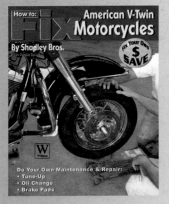

Choppers don't have to cost $30,000. In fact, a chopper built from the right parts can be assembled for as little as $5,000. How to Build a Cheap Chopper documents the construction of 4 inexpensive choppers with complete start-to-finish sequences photographed in the shops of Donnie Smith, Brian Klock and Dave Perewitz.

Least expensive is the metric chopper, based on a Japanese 4-cylinder engine and transmission installed in a hardtail frame. Next up, price wise, are 2 bikes built using Buell/Sportster drivetrains. The recipe here is simple; combine one used Buell or Sportster with a hardtail frame for an almost instant chopper. The big twin chopper is the least cheap of the 4, yet it's still far less expensive than most bikes built today. Cheap Chopper uses 144 pages and over 400 color images to completely explain each assembly.

| Eleven Chapters | 144 Pages | $27.95 | Over 400 photos, 100% color |

HOW TO FIX AMERICAN V-TWIN MOTORCYCLES

Ownership of a modern American Motorcycle – no matter how good it is – requires certain mechanical skills. This book from Wolfgang Publications covers all the skills needed to do basic maintenance and repairs on your American motorcycle.

From adjusting the clutch cable to installing brake pads, this book explains in both words and photos how to safely do your own work. Instead of taking the bike back to the dealer or shop where you bought it, roll it into your garage and do it yourself.

When you're trying to learn something for the first time, there's nothing like a good photo, or series of photos, that show exactly how the operation is performed. There is no such thing as a maintenance free motorcycle. Save money and gain satisfaction. Learn how to do your own repairs in your own small shop with this book from Wolfgang Publications.

| Eleven Chapters | 144 Pages | $27.95 | Over 350 photos, 100% color |

TATTOO BIBLE - BOOK TWO

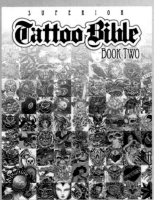

Based on the success of Tattoo Bible - Book One, ArtKulture Publishing brings to market Tattoo Bible - Book Two, another unique and colorful collection of flash art. Everything is here, from Skulls to Tribal, Americana to the avant-garde.

Tattoo Bible includes flash images never before compiled in one single book. The artists included in this book include the very well known, and those artists who should be well known. The best known names include Kevin LeBlanc, Aaron Coleman, Bob Sims, Nate Powers and many, many more.

Tattoo Bible - Book Two, covers different styles and an endless supply of ideas. Make your own design by combining different pieces of art from within the book, or use one of the images as a stand-alone tattoo. Let this book be a supplement to your imagination.

| 144 Pages | $27.95 | Over 500 pieces of flash art, 100% color |

Wolfgang Publication Titles

For a current list visit our website at www.wolfpub.com

ILLUSTRATED HISTORY

Triumph Motorcycles	$32.95

BIKER BASICS

Sheet Metal Fabrication	$27.95
How to FIX American V-Twin MC	$27.95

COMPOSITE GARAGE

Composite Materials Handbook #1	$27.95
Composite Materials Handbook #2	$27.95

HOP-UP EXPERT

How to Hop & Customize Your Bagger	$27.95
How to Hop & Customize Your Softail	$27.95

OLD SKOOL SKILLS

Barris: Grilles,Scoops, Fins and Frenching (Vol. 2)	$24.95
Barris: Flames Scallops, Paneling and Striping (Vol. 4)	$24.95

HOT ROD BASICS

How to Air Condition Your Hot Rod	$27.95
How to Chop Tops	$24.95

MOTORCYCLE RESTORATION SERIES

Triumph Resotoration - Unit 650cc	$29.95
Triumph MC Restoration Pre-Unit	$29.95
Harley-Davidson Panhead Restoration	$34.95

AIR SKOOL SKILLS

How Airbrushes Work	$27.95
How to Airbrush Pin-Ups	$27.95
Air Brushing 101	$27.95
Airbrush Bible	$27.95

PAINT EXPERT

Advanced Custom Motorcycle Painting	$27.95
Advanced Airbrush Art	$27.95
Advanced Custom Painting Techniques	$27.95
Advanced Pinstripe Art	$27.95
Kustom Painting Secrets	$19.95
Custom Paint & Graphics	$27.95
Pro Airbrush Techniques	$27.95
Pro Pinstripe Techniques	$27.95

SHEET METAL

Advanced Sheet Metal Fabrication	$27.95
Ultimate Sheet Metal Fabrication	$24.95
Sheet Metal Bible	$29.95

CUSTOM BUILDER SERIES

Advanced Custom Motorcycle Wiring	$27.95
Advanced Custom Motorcycle Assembly & Fabrication	$27.95
Advanced Custom Motorcycle Chassis	$27.95
How to Build a Cheap Chopper	$27.95
How to Build a Chopper	$27.95

TATTOO U Series

Body Painting	$27.95
Tattoo- From Idea to Ink	$27.95
Tattoos Behind the Needle	$27.95
Advanced Tattoo Art	$27.95
Tattoo Bible Book One	$27.95
Tattoo Bible Book Two	$27.95

HOME SHOP

How to Paint Tractors & Trucks	$27.95

NOTEWORTHY

Guitar Building Basics	
Acoustic Assembly at Home	$27.95

AUGUST 1 - 14, 2011
ON SALE NOW
STURGIS 71ST
EARLY BIRD PRICING!

BROKEN SPOKE
CAMPGROUND

Broken Spoke Saloon

- HUGE POOL W/HOT TUBS & TIKI BAR
- OVERSIZE RV SPOTS W/FULL HOOK-UPS
- LIVE MUSIC DAY & NIGHT - FREE FOR CAMPERS!
- JOHNNY "CHOP" HILL CLIMB
- ENORMOUS RIDE-THRU BROKEN SPOKE SALOON
- GOOD OL' DAYS RACEWAY (1/4 MI DIRT TRACK)
- GENERAL STORE WITH WI-FI, GROCERIES, CAMPING SUPPLIES & MORE!
- PRIVATE CABINS W/ A/C, FRIDGE & MICROWAVE
- ROLLING PARTY BUS
- HOT, PRIVATE SHOWERS
- LIMPNICKIE LOT
- COIN-OP LAUNDRY
- DAILY BIKER BLOODY MARY BUFFET BREAKFAST

BROKEN SPOKE
CAMPGROUND
79 NORTH · STURGIS SD

Pool Parties!!!
Aug 1 - 14, 2011
Camper Amenities in Sturgis

NORTH 79

WWW.BROKENSPOKECAMPGROUND.COM
CALL TOLL FREE:
877-653-6679 (8-SPOKE-ON-79)

THE LEGENDARY
BUFFALO CHIP
©2009 BUFFALO CHIP CAMPGROUND, LLC.

BEST PARTY ANYWHERE

WWW.BUFFALOCHIP.COM

GET YOUR OFFICIAL BUFFALO CHIP MERCHANDISE AT: **HOT LEATHERS**.com

Are you interested in selling the Anniversary book?

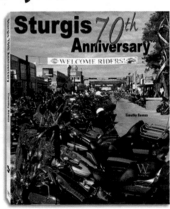

Dealers and shops can buy these Sturgis Anniversary books at a significant discount, and get a free counter rack at the same time.

Just call Tim or Krista at 651-275-0198 or send an email to info@wolfpub.com.

wolfgang publications

The First Fifty Years
Limited Offer - Only a few books remain

A look at the first fifty years of Sturgis, including "The Big One" in 1990. Many historic photos and interviews with the guys who started it all - the Jackpine Gypsies. Only a few books remain from the original run of this classic. First come, first served.
Only $19.95 - FREE SHIPPING.

Send Check or MO to:

**Mike Urseth
N14321-705th Street
New Auburn, WI
54757**